The Dominican Kitchen

The Dominican Kitchen

Homestyle Recipes That Celebrate the Flavors, Traditions, and Culture of the Dominican Republic

VANESSA MOTA

ROCK
POINT

Brimming with creative inspiration, how-to projects, and useful information to enrich your everyday life, quarto.com is a favorite destination for those pursuing their interests and passions.

First published in 2023 by Rock Point, an imprint of The Quarto Group,
142 West 36th Street, 4th Floor, New York, NY 10018, USA
T (212) 779-4972 F (212) 779-6058 www.Quarto.com

Rock Point titles are also available at discount for retail, wholesale, promotional and bulk purchase. For details, contact the Special Sales Manager by email at specialsales@quarto.com or by mail at The Quarto Group, Attn: Special Sales Manager, 100 Cummings Center Suite, 265D, Beverly, MA 01915, USA.

10 9 8 7 6 5 4 3 2 1

ISBN: 978-1-63106-887-4

Library of Congress Control Number: 2022945438

Publisher: Rage Kindelsperger
Creative Director: Laura Drew
Editorial Director: Erin Canning
Managing Editor: Cara Donaldson
Cover Illustration: Marisa Kwek
Interior Design: Lisa Berman
Photography: Aneudy Rosado (pp. 13, 179), Jenny Clater (p. 176, top left), and Jayden Rosado (p. 208)

Printed in China

To my dear mom,
who is my biggest supporter.

And to my children,
the best food critics in the world.

contents

main dishes 99

desserts 149

drinks 177

✕✕✕✕✕✕✕✕✕ introduction ✕✕✕✕✕✕✕✕✕✕

As a child or even as a young adult, I was never very interested in cooking; however, most of my happiest memories as a kid are directly connected to food. Growing up in my beloved Dominican Republic, I learned firsthand what it truly means to share a meal and connect with others through food. My mornings began with a trip to the farmers market with my mom to buy ingredients for the day's meals. We would walk around visiting different vendors to find the best-quality ingredients. I would watch my mom handpick each one of the items on the list given to her by my grandmother.

After we returned home, I would attentively watch my grandmother cook the day's lunch with the ingredients we had just bought and then set the table for everyone to enjoy lunch together as a family. She would often make plátanos maduros (fried sweet plantains) because she knew it was (and still is) my favorite side dish. Some afternoons, she would sit on the front porch of the house and shell the pigeon peas she had bought from one of the street vendors that drove around the neighborhood selling fruits and vegetables. I would sometimes sit with her and help. She taught me how to remove the pigeon peas from the shell and pick out the ones that didn't look good. She would then clean and save the good ones for the next day's lunch.

My grandmother was not a very expressive woman, but through her, I learned that cooking is a love language. I learned that you should always cook a little extra to have leftovers. I also learned that if anyone arrives unexpectedly during lunch or dinnertime, they should be immediately invited to sit at the table. "A buen tiempo" (In good time), she'd say, a joyous and sincere phrase that invites people to share a meal. That is the Dominican way.

Whether it's with a big pot of sancocho (meat and vegetable stew) to feed a crowd or the famous empaguetadas (Dominican spaghetti), even a group school project meeting turns into a culinary event. If there's one thing to know about Dominicans, it's that no matter where we are or what we're doing, three things characterize us: we cook, we party, and we eat. Every occasion is a celebration.

It's not a surprise, then, that as an adult I use food to build memories with those whom I love. But it wasn't always that way. For starters, I didn't learn how to cook until later in adulthood, after getting married and being pregnant with my first child. It was then that I started craving the homemade meals my grandmother and mom used to make. And although I was always around food and watched them cook growing up, I never learned how to cook myself.

It was then that my quest to learn how to cook las comidas de mi tierra (the foods from my land) started. The challenge was that my grandmother and extended family were more than fifteen hundred miles away, and though my mom was closer, she worked all day. After numerous mishaps, trials, and errors, and working through the "a pinch of this and a bit of that" instructions provided by my family members over the phone, I was able to start cooking the recipes I had missed.

In 2014, I started a blog sharing my recipes in the hope that it would help anyone going through a similar situation as mine and missing the meals they grew up eating. I also wanted to create an organized collection of recipes that my children could use in the future. Over time, I began receiving emails and messages on social media from people saying how much a particular recipe reminded them of home or of the moment when they first tasted the recipe.

I have developed many of the recipes I share. Some of them are my mom's recipes, which she cooked with me while I took the liberty to measure and weigh every single ingredient with the purpose of writing it down. And others are adaptations from the recipes given to me by family members.

Few things have the power to unite people as food does. There's a level of comfort and joy that surrounds us when we share a meal with someone. Plenty of laughs and deep conversations take place around the dinner table, creating moments and experiences that are undeniably priceless.

This cookbook is a collection of everyday Dominican meals, and my hope is that it serves as a resource for people who want to learn how to prepare the comida criolla (Creole food) they grew up eating, but might no longer have access to the recipes due to migration or loss of those family members who were the keepers of such treasures. It is also for those who want to pass down these recipes to their children and family members but are still working with a pinch of this and a bit of that, unsure as to the true measurements of the ingredients other than love.

Happy cooking and ¡buen provecho!

Most of the ingredients in a Dominican pantry are common items found at grocery stores in the United States. A few ingredients are not as common outside the island, although they can often be found in grocery stores in areas with a high Dominican population, such as New York City, and even in the ethnic foods section of grocery stores elsewhere. The recipes in this book are all prepared using these common ingredients with a few exceptions for specific ingredients that can be purchased online and shipped if you can't find them in your area. Here, I've listed the essential ingredients to keep in your pantry or refrigerator to help you create wonderfully flavored Dominican dishes.

fruits & vegetables

AVOCADOS (AGUACATES) In the Dominican Republic, we use tropical avocados, which are bigger than Mexican ones, have a high water content and buttery texture, and are mild in flavor. They are used for making Ensalada de Aguacate (page 51) and Pan con Aguacate (page 41). They are often served simply sliced as a side with many other meals, such as soups and stews.

BELL PEPPERS (PIMIENTO MORRÓN) Bell peppers of any color are an important part of Dominican cuisine and are used in most of our dishes with a sofrito base.

BITTER ORANGES (NARANJAS AGRIAS) Bitter orange juice is used in Dominican cooking to marinate meat and provide a distinctive citrus flavor to a variety of dishes. The oranges taste sour and have a thick, rough skin. The fresh fruit is sold at Hispanic grocery stores and many Hispanic product brands also sell bottled bitter orange juice.

CABBAGE (REPOLLO) Green cabbage is a favorite for making salads and an important ingredient in recipes such as Chimichurri (Chimi) Burgers (page 42) and niño envuelto.

CARIBBEAN SWEET POTATOES (BATATAS) In the United States, this type of sweet potato is known as boniato and can be distinguished by its rusty-red skin and creamy white flesh. In the Dominican Republic, batatas are fried (page 78) and served as a side dish and also used in desserts such as Jalea (page 155) and Habichuelas con Dulce (page 152).

CASSAVA (YUCA) The starchy, fibrous, edible root of the cassava plant, this vegetable, along with rice and corn, is a popular source of carbohydrates in tropical countries. In the United States, the long, brown roots are waxed and sold in the produce section of grocery stores. It is also available frozen, peeled, and cut into chunks or grated. You can also find it with the ethnic foods in the freezer section of the grocery store.

CELERY (APIO) Celery is used as a flavoring agent for dishes such as soups and stews.

COCONUT (COCO) On a tropical island where coconuts grow wild, it is natural to see this fruit take center stage in many Dominican dishes. The milk is extracted from the coconut and used in many sweet and savory dishes. The flesh is also grated and used in a variety of desserts and baked goods. Despite the benefits of using fresh coconut, canned coconut milk and packaged shredded coconut are recommended for ease of use for the recipes in this book, except for Jalao (page 161), which requires fresh shredded coconut.

CUBANELLE PEPPERS (AJÍES CUBANELA)
These bright light-green peppers are sweet and can be interchanged with bell peppers in many recipes.

GARLIC Garlic is used in almost every dish in some form or another. It plays a pivotal role in sofrito seasoning and Wasakaka Sauce (page 133).

GINGER In its fresh form, ginger is used to flavor many desserts and make a tasty tea (page 196).

GUINEITOS Guineitos are green, unripe bananas that are typically boiled and served as a savory side dish (page 77).

KABOCHA SQUASH (AUYAMA) This type of winter squash, with a speckled, dark-green skin, is commonly used in Dominican cooking to add flavor and body to soups and stews. It is also enjoyed boiled and mashed with a bit of butter.

LIMES Dominicans use limes in a variety of ways. Lime juice is used to make Morir Soñando (page 90). It is also used to marinate meat and seafood and flavor salad dressings. Lime peel is used in a number of Dominican desserts as a flavor agent. One lime can yield between 1 and 2 tablespoons of lime juice, depending on its size.

ONIONS Red onions are the most common type of onion used in almost every dish in the Dominican Republic. They play an important role in the tomato-based sofrito sauce that serves as a base for many dishes. Dominicans also love to sauté onions with vinegar to use as a garnish in many dishes, such as Mangú (page 101), Yuca con Cebolla (page 72), and a number of meat dishes.

PLANTAINS Both green and yellow plantains are a staple in a Dominican kitchen. This ingredient forms an important part of Dominican cuisine and has become a symbol of dominicanidad (being Dominican). Plantains resemble large bananas in appearance; however, they must be cooked and not eaten raw, unlike bananas. Green plantains are more difficult to peel and have a starchy texture like potatoes. (See page 21 for directions on how to peel plantains.) They are great for savory recipes such as Mangú (page 101). Yellow plantains, on the other hand, are ripened plantains. They are soft and sweet and work well in sweet dishes such as Plátanos al Caldero (page 157) and savory dishes such as Pastelón de Plátano Maduro (page 113). Both types are used to make Plátanos Fritos (page 75), which are often served as part of Dominican meals.

SWEET PEPPERS (AJÍES GUSTOSOS)
Sweet peppers are used to season a variety of dishes. They are small and sweet wtih a slightly smoky flavor and a zesty undertone—similar to habanero peppers but without the spiciness. These peppers aren't widely available in the United States, so I substitute with cubanelle peppers (4 sweet peppers equal 1 medium cubanelle pepper) or simply leave this ingredient out of a recipe if I can't find it.

YAUTÍA This root vegetable is commonly used for Sancocho Dominicano (page 85), along with cassava and plantains. There are three types of yautía—white, yellow, and purple—and all are used the same way, although their flavors vary slightly.

herbs & spices

ALLSPICE (MALAGUETA) Known in the United States as allspice, it is mostly used for seasoning soups in the Dominican Republic. For the recipes in this book, use whole allspice.

ANNATTO (BIJA) Also known as achiote, annatto is used for coloring foods red. Because of its unique, mild flavor, annatto is also used as a seasoning without dramatically altering the flavor of the food. You can find it in powdered form or use the seeds to make achiote oil by heating the seeds in oil over low heat to extract the color. For the recipes in this book, use the powdered type.

ANISE SEED (ANÍS) Anise seed is mainly used to cook Arepitas (pages 25 and 26), Chulitos (page 30), and Pan de Yuca (page 37). These aromatic seeds have a strong, sweet licorice flavor, and a little bit goes a long way.

CILANTRO Fresh cilantro is a main ingredient in Dominican sazón (seasoning), which is used to marinate meats, and in a number of other dishes such as Habichuelas Guisadas (page 63) and most rice dishes. To keep it fresh longer, cut the ends and place it in a jar with water in the refrigerator.

CINNAMON (CANELA) Cinnamon is used in a variety of desserts and beverages such as Majarete (page 162), Chocolate Caliente (page 195), and herbal teas. Both cinnamon sticks and powdered cinnamon are must-haves.

CLOVES CLAVO (DULCE) Like cinnamon, cloves are an important spice when making Dominican desserts. They are used in Habichuelas con Dulce (page 152), Arroz con Leche (page 158), and Plátanos al Caldero (page 157).

CULANTRO (CILANTRO ANCHO) In the Dominican Republic, this fresh herb is commonly known as cilantro ancho; in the United States and other Latin American countries, it's known as culantro. It has long, thin leaves with serrated edges. Culantro tastes stronger than cilantro and is best when cooked, as it releases more flavor. Dominicans use it in soups and stews such as Sancocho Dominicano (page 85) and Sopa de Pico y Pala (page 90).

DOMINICAN OREGANO One of the most commonly used herbs in Dominican cooking is dried Dominican oregano. Dominican oregano has a stronger flavor than the more common Italian oregano available in grocery stores. For authentic flavor, I recommend always using Dominican oregano while preparing Dominican food. For the recipes in this book, use the dried-leaf type.

NUTMEG (NUEZ MOSCADA) Along with cinnamon and cloves, nutmeg is used in a number of Dominican desserts and beverages. It's also added to coffee for flavor—my grandmother never drank coffee without it. For the freshest flavor, buy whole nutmeg that you can grate, if possible.

SALT AND BLACK PEPPER Both are used as basic flavoring agents in the Dominican Republic, and most savory recipes in this book call for them.

meat, fish & dairy

BACALAO Bacalao is cod that has been dried and salted to preserve it. This method of preservation has been used since ancient times, allowing the food to become a valuable commodity in international trade. As a result, the ingredient spread around the Atlantic and became a staple in the cuisines of many Northern European, Mediterranean, West African, and Caribbean countries. Before cooking, the fish must be rehydrated. This can be achieved by soaking it in cold water overnight and changing the water two or three times, or soaking it for a few hours and then boiling it for about 15 minutes in plenty of water. This process also removes some of the salt.

DOMINICAN SALAMI Dominican salami is a popular and inexpensive protein option in the Dominican Republic. It's a type of cured sausage, smoked and salted, made of pork or beef and seasoned with a combination of spices typical in Dominican cooking, such as garlic, black pepper, and Dominican oregano. It's more likely to be found in a store that specializes in Hispanic foods. I purchase it from the cold cuts section of my local grocer. If you can't find it locally, you can get it online.

DOMINICAN SAUSAGE (LONGANIZA) In Dominican cuisine, this thin pork sausage is typically fried or cooked to a mild crispness to make Locrio de Longaniza (page 105) or to serve with Mangú (page 101). It also goes well with Plátanos Fritos (page 75), Batatas Fritas (page 78), or any other side dish.

QUESO DE FREÍR This particular type of cheese has a high melting point, which makes it perfect for frying. It is usually served with the beloved Dominican dish Mangú (page 101) and can be found in the dairy section at grocery stores.

dry ingredients, canned goods & fats

ALCAPARRADO This mix of green olives, pimiento strips, and capers is a common condiment used in casseroles, meat, and rice dishes. You can substitute with pimiento-stuffed green olives if alcaparrado is not available to you.

BEANS Beans are a staple of Dominican cuisine. Red, black, pinto, white, Roman, and fava (havas) beans are among our favorites. Red beans are especially well liked and used in dishes such as Moro de Habichuelas Rojas (page 67) and Habichuelas Guisadas (page 63). Some of the recipes in the book call for canned beans while others use dried beans.

BOUILLON TABLETS (CHICKEN OR VEGETABLE) Bouillon tablets are typically used in Dominican homes as a substitute for chicken or vegetable broth. Also available in granulated form, bouillon has a long shelf life and can be used in many recipes that range from soups and stews to rice and meat dishes. Chicken bouillon is also known as caldo de pollo.

BULGUR (TRIGO) Bulgur wheat is a Middle Eastern ingredient that has become an important part of Dominican cuisine. Dominicans use bulgur in a number of ways, and it is the main ingredient to make Kipes (page 34).

COCONUT MILK Canned unsweetened coconut milk is used as a substitute for fresh coconut milk extracted from the coconut. This is an easier and quicker way to add coconut flavor to recipes. It also has a longer shelf life.

CORNMEAL Dominicans use cornmeal in both sweet and savory dishes. From baked goods to fritters and pastelón (casseroles), this ingredient is a staple in a Dominican kitchen.

EVAPORATED MILK Because of the long shelf life of evaporated milk and its many uses, it is deemed one of those ingredients you should always keep in your pantry. It is used in desserts and beverages such as Morir Soñando (page 179).

continued on following page

continued from previous page

LONG-GRAIN WHITE RICE Rice is a staple ingredient in Dominican homes, and most meals are either cooked with rice or served with rice as a side dish. Long-grain white rice is preferred, as it is light and dry when cooked and doesn't stick together.

OIL (CORN, VEGETABLE, AND OLIVE) Corn oil is the preferred option for cooking and frying meats in the Dominican Republic. Vegetable oil is also used for cooking in general, and what I prefer to use. Good-quality olive oil is mostly used for making salad dressings.

PIGEON PEAS (GANDULES) Pigeon peas are a popular legume in the Caribbean. Fresh pigeon peas come in a shell, like beans, and need to be peeled before cooking, which in some cases can be therapeutic and a bit of a pastime. They can also be bought canned and frozen at grocery stores. Arroz con gandules is a popular dish made with this ingredient, as is Moro de Gandules con Coco (page 68).

SHREDDED COCONUT This sweetened dried coconut is used in Dominican desserts and baked goods, as well as for garnish.

TOMATO SAUCE OR PASTE This is generally used for flavor and to add color to dishes. Many Dominican dishes have a tomato-based sofrito sauce in which tomato sauce or paste is used.

tools & equipment

XXXXXXXX **tools & equipment** XXXXXXXX

The recipes in this cookbook can be prepared with tools and equipment you already have in your kitchen, with the exception of a few items that can help ensure the proper preparation of a dish with ease.

CALDERO A caldero is a cast-aluminum pot that is the main kitchen tool in a Dominican home. These pots are sturdy, conduct heat well, and are quite durable. Calderos are used to simmer stews and soups, as well as to cook rice and beans, braise meats, and fry your favorite foods. Personally, I have never tasted a bad Concón (page 60) that was made in one of these.

MORTAR AND PESTLE (PILÓN) This tool is used to crush, grind, or mash ingredients, such as garlic and spices. It is made in different styles in a variety of materials such as wood, aluminum, and stone. In Dominican homes, a pilón is typically used to pound garlic into a paste before adding it to a recipe. If you don't have a mortar and pestle, you can finely mince the garlic or pulse it in a food processor until it turns into a coarse paste.

ROLLING PIN In Dominican cooking, rolling pins are mostly used for making Yaniqueques (page 38) and Pastelitos (page 29), in which the dough needs to be rolled out and cut into discs before being filled and fried.

SACKCLOTH KITCHEN TOWELS OR CHEESECLOTH To avoid any accidents with excess spatter when frying, we use a sackcloth towel or cheesecloth to squeeze the surplus liquid from grated cassava and soaked bulgur wheat before preparing Chulitos (page 30) and Kipes (page 34).

TOSTONERA A tostonera is a tool made of bamboo that is used to mash fried plantains to make Tostones (page 76). There are different types of tostoneras. The traditional tostonera presses a plantain into a flat circle. There is also a deep tostonera, which presses the plantains into a cup for stuffing for Tostones Rellenos (page 117). This is a neat tool to have but not necessary, because you can flatten the plantains with a small dish or saucepan, bottle, or glass.

✕✕✕✕✕✕✕✕✕ what is sofrito? ✕✕✕✕✕✕✕✕✕

You will see sofrito referenced throughout the recipes in this book. Sofrito is a mixture of aromatic ingredients mainly used in Spanish and Latin American cooking. Dominicans often refer to sofrito as sazón, and many Dominican dishes call for it as the main seasoning element. It's used as the base for our salsa criolla (Creole sauce), which is found in most of our guisos (stews), meat dishes, and even Espaguetis Dominicanos (page 114). Tomato sauce or paste is added to the sofrito to make this delicious sauce. Some of the ingredients used in sofrito include peppers, onions, garlic, cilantro, culantro (cilantro ancho), sweet peppers (ajíes gustosos), Dominican oregano, and, in some instances, chopped plum tomato. The ingredients added to the sofrito depend on individual preference, and each recipe varies from home to home. To save on cooking time, you can process your sofrito ingredients together in a food processor or blender until they are chopped and have obtained a uniform texture. Transfer the mixture to an airtight container and refrigerate for up to 2 weeks. You can also freeze it in portions for up to 3 months in an ice-cube tray, with each cube containing 2 tablespoons of sofrito. This is convenient because you can then drop a cube in stews and soups, such as Sancocho Dominicano (page 85), or rice dishes, such as Locrio de Pollo (page 102).

sazón dominicano

YIELD 4 cups (960 g)   **PREP TIME** 15 minutes

1 bunch fresh cilantro, roughly chopped

1 bunch fresh culantro (cilantro ancho), roughly chopped

2 large green bell peppers, cut in quarters and seeds removed

3 medium red onions, cut in quarters

20 cloves garlic

8 sweet peppers (ajíes gustosos), cut in half and seeds removed

2 tablespoons dried Dominican oregano (optional)

1 Place all the ingredients in a food processor or blender and process until all ingredients are chopped and have obtained a uniform texture. Pulse the ingredients as you add them to the food processor to start breaking them down so that it all fits.

2 Transfer to an airtight container, cover with a lid, and store in the refrigerator for up to 2 weeks or place 2-tablespoon portions in ice-cube trays and freeze for up to 3 months.

note *If you can't find sweet peppers, use 2 medium cubanelle peppers or leave this ingredient out.*

✕✕✕✕✕✕✕ how to peel plantains ✕✕✕✕✕✕✕

Plantains are one of my favorite ingredients in Dominican cooking. They can be used to make a variety of delectable recipes, both sweet and savory. Green plantains are best for savory dishes, while ripe sweet (yellow) plantains can be used for both savory and sweet dishes.

Plantains that are ripe are slightly firm to the touch and primarily yellow with some black spots. The plantain becomes riper and sweeter as the skin darkens. Unripe plantains are identified by their green exterior. An important thing about plantains is that they must always be cooked and not eaten raw.

Before you can cook some scrumptious Plátanos Fritos (page 75), you must first learn how to peel them.

1. Cut the ends off the plantains, then carefully slide your knife lengthwise down one side of the peel without cutting into the flesh, and then again on the opposite side.

2. Set the knife down and use your fingers to separate and detach the plantain's peel. Repeat these steps to remove the rest of the skin. Peeling ripe (yellow) plantains is much easier than green ones. After running your knife through the skin without cutting into the flesh, the skin will simply peel off like a banana peel.

Be sure that the plantains are at room temperature so that it is easier to peel them. If you keep your plantains in the fridge and need to peel them in a rush, place them in a bowl with hot water for about 5 to 10 minutes to warm them up, then proceed with peeling.

Peeling Yellow Plaintains

  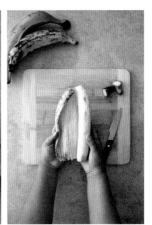

Peeling Green Plaintains

XXXXXXXXXXXXXXXXXXXXXXXX

snacks
&
sandwiches

Handheld fried snacks and meat-filled sandwiches are emblems of Dominican street-food fare. They also make for delicious appetizers, perfect to enjoy before a homemade meal or to serve at a party. The easy recipes in this chapter include my tried-and-true arepitas de yuca; a favorite beachside snack, yaniqueques; and the king at Dominican food trucks, the chimichurri burger. And don't forget the stars of the Dominican picadera: kipes, chulitos, and pastelitos.

arepitas de maíz
cornmeal fritters

YIELD 12 to 14 arepitas   PREP TIME 5 minutes   COOK TIME 15 minutes

This recipe is inspired by the arepitas de maíz I first had at a street-corner Dominican bodega in Bushwick, Brooklyn. As a teenager, I remember walking to the bodega after school to buy a snack to take home. Instead of browsing the store aisles for chips and cookies as the other kids did, I would head straight to the buffet-style food section, where I would always pick up two arepitas de maíz and a Morir Soñando (page 179). Ramona, the cook at the bodega, would set the arepitas aside for me in case they sold out before I came by to pick up mine. She made her cornmeal fritters in their simplest form. I've adjusted the recipe to add sweet corn, onion, and cilantro, which add texture and great fresh flavor.

1 cup (180 g) fine yellow cornmeal

¼ cup (50 g) granulated sugar

1 teaspoon butter, softened

1 large egg, lightly beaten

½ teaspoon salt

½ cup (120 ml) lukewarm water

2 tablespoons canned sweet corn kernels, drained

1 tablespoon finely chopped red onion

1 tablespoon finely chopped fresh cilantro

1 cup (240 ml) corn or vegetable oil, for frying

1. In a medium bowl, mix the cornmeal, sugar, butter, and egg until well combined.

2. In a small bowl, add the salt to the lukewarm water, then slowly mix it into the cornmeal mixture.

3. Stir in the corn, onion, and cilantro.

4. In a medium skillet, heat the oil over medium heat. Once the oil is hot, add the mixture, 1 tablespoon at a time, flattening it into small, thick pancakes. Fry for 2 to 3 minutes on each side, or until golden brown. You may need to cook in batches.

5. Transfer the fritters to a plate lined with paper towels to remove excess oil.

6. Serve warm.

arepitas de yuca
cassava fritters

YIELD 16 to 18 arepitas   **PREP TIME** 10 minutes   **COOK TIME** 15 minutes

Arepitas de yuca is one of the first dishes I ever cooked. My love for the savory appetizer was such that I would prepare it for every gathering or event I hosted, and the dish was always received with much delight by my guests. The crispy cassava fritter is infused with aromatic anise seed and the subtle taste of mild cheddar cheese.

2 pounds (907 g) fresh cassava (yuca), peeled and grated (see Note)

1 tablespoon butter, softened

1 large egg, beaten

1 teaspoon anise seed

1 teaspoon salt

½ teaspoon granulated sugar (see Note)

¼ cup (30 g) shredded mild cheddar cheese (optional)

1 cup (240 ml) vegetable or corn oil, for frying

1. In a medium bowl, mix the cassava, butter, egg, anise seed, salt, sugar, and cheese (if using) until well combined.

2. In a medium skillet, heat the oil over medium heat. Once the oil is hot, add the mixture, 1 tablespoon at a time, flattening it a bit. Fry for 2 to 3 minutes on each side, or until golden brown and cooked through. You may need to cook in batches.

3. Transfer the fritters to a plate lined with paper towels to remove excess oil.

4. Serve warm.

note
You can also use frozen shredded cassava and add it with the other ingredients in the first step. I add a little sugar to the fritter mixture to help remove the bitterness casava can sometimes have.

note

The pastelitos can be prepared in advance, up to the point of frying them, and frozen for up to 4 weeks. Make sure to completely thaw the pastelitos in the refrigerator before frying to avoid spatter.

pastelitos de pollo
mini chicken empanadas

YIELD 16 pastelitos	PREP TIME 30 minutes, plus 30 minutes' rest time	COOK TIME 20 minutes

Pastelitos are the Dominican version of the empanada, and they're a must-have item on the picadera (snack platter) at any fiesta. Perfectly portable, they are a popular appetizer made with a flour dough that can be filled many different ways, often using leftovers such as Ground Beef Filling (page 47) or Masa de Cangrejo Guisado (page 142). In this variation, I use a filling of shredded chicken cooked in a tomato-based sofrito sauce.

pastelitos de pollo

2 cups (250 g) all-purpose flour, plus more for dusting

1 teaspoon salt

1 tablespoon granulated sugar

¼ cup (55 g) unsalted butter, softened

1 large egg, lightly beaten

1 recipe Shredded Chicken Filling (page 46)

3 cups (720 ml) corn or vegetable oil, for frying

mayo-ketchup sauce (optional)

3 tablespoons mayonnaise

1½ tablespoons ketchup

½ teaspoon garlic powder

1. To make the pastelitos de pollo: In a large bowl, stir together the flour, salt, and sugar. Add the butter and, using your hands, combine the flour mixture with the butter. Add the egg and continue mixing with your hands to combine well.

2. Slowly pour in ½ cup (120 ml) of water, a little bit at a time, while working the dough with your hands. Continue working the dough for about 5 minutes, or until all the ingredients are incorporated and the dough does not stick to your hands.

3. Cover the bowl with a clean kitchen towel and let rest for at least 30 minutes.

4. To assemble the pastelitos, separate the dough into 4 equal-size pieces. Using a rolling pin, roll one of the pieces on a lightly floured surface to ¼ inch (6 mm) thick. Cut out as many pastry rounds as possible using a 3-inch (7.5 cm) round cutter or glass. Add 1 tablespoon of the chicken filling to the center of a pastry round and top with another pastry round. Press firmly around the edges with a fork to seal and transfer to a baking sheet or floured board. Repeat this step with the remaining dough and filling, rerolling the dough scraps for more rounds (see Note).

5. In a medium pot, heat the oil over medium heat. Once the oil is hot, fry the pastelitos, in batches, for 2 to 3 minutes on each side, or until golden brown.

6. Transfer the pastelitos to a plate lined with paper towels to remove excess oil.

7. To make the mayo-ketchup sauce (if using): In a small bowl, mix the mayonnaise, ketchup, and garlic powder until well combined.

8. Serve warm with the mayo-ketchup sauce (if using) on the side.

chulitos
cassava rolls

YIELD 12 chulitos   **PREP TIME** 15 minutes   **COOK TIME** 15 minutes

When we talk about street-food fare, chulitos are near the top of the list. In the Dominican Republic, it's not uncommon to pass by street vendors along the side of the road and see an extra-large pot filled with oil over a charcoal anafe (portable stove), ready to cook this delightful finger food. These delicious rolls are made with yuca (cassava) and often filled with cheese, like here, or Ground Beef (page 47) for chulitos de carne, and then deep-fried.

chulitos

2 pounds (907 g) fresh cassava (yuca), peeled and grated

1 tablespoon butter, softened

1 large egg, beaten

½ teaspoon adobo seasoning

1 teaspoon granulated sugar

½ teaspoon anise seed

¼ teaspoon salt

1 cup (115 g) shredded mild cheddar cheese (about 4 ounces)

2 to 3 cups (480 to 720 ml) vegetable or corn oil, for deep-frying

creamy cilantro sauce (optional)

½ cup roughly chopped fresh cilantro

1 tablespoon mayonnaise

1 clove garlic

Juice of ½ lime

1 tablespoon olive oil

1 tablespoon apple cider vinegar

Pinch salt

1 To make the chulitos: Squeeze the grated cassava with a clean sackcloth towel or cheesecloth to remove excess liquid.

2 In a medium bowl, mix the cassava, butter, egg, adobo, sugar, anise seed, and salt until well combined.

3 Place about 2 tablespoons of the cassava mixture in the palm of your hand and flatten it. Place 1 tablespoon of cheese in the center and roll the mixture around the cheese with your hands to seal it. Make sure to cover the cheese well with the cassava mixture so that it doesn't ooze out when frying and transfer to a baking sheet. Repeat this step with the remaining cassava mixture and cheese.

4 In a medium pot, heat enough oil to cover the chulitos by ½ inch (12 mm) over medium-high heat (see Note). Once the oil is hot, deep-fry the chulitos, in batches, for 3 to 4 minutes on each side, or until golden brown.

5 Transfer the chulitos to a plate lined with paper towels to remove excess oil.

6 To make the creamy cilantro sauce (if using): Add all the ingredients to a food processor or a blender and process until smooth.

7 Serve warm with the creamy cilantro sauce (if using) on the side.

note

The oil should be hot when you fry the chulitos. You can drop a little of the mixture into the oil to check that it is hot enough—it should sizzle and form bubbles around the mixture if it is ready.

note

Peeling the eggplant is optional; you can leave it on if desired.

torrejas de berenjenas
fried eggplant

YIELD 4 servings   PREP TIME 10 minutes   COOK TIME 15 minutes

In the Dominican Republic, there's a common saying that goes "cuando hay berenjena no hace falta carne" (when there is eggplant you don't need meat). For as long as I can remember, eggplant has been the preferred substitution for meat among Dominicans. This fried eggplant recipe is a vegetarian favorite that can be served as an appetizer or as a meat substitute for the main dish.

1½ cups (360 ml) vegetable oil, for deep-frying

2 large eggs, beaten

¼ cup (35 g) finely chopped onion

½ teaspoon salt

¼ teaspoon ground black pepper

1 pound (454 g) eggplant, peeled and cut into ½-inch (12 mm) slices (see Note)

1. In a large skillet, heat the oil over medium heat.

2. In a shallow dish, mix the eggs, onion, salt, and pepper until well combined. Coat the eggplant slices thoroughly on both sides with the egg mixture.

3. Deep-fry the eggplant, in batches, for 3 to 4 minutes on each side, or until cooked through and golden brown.

4. Transfer the eggplant to a plate lined with paper towels to remove excess oil.

5. Serve warm.

kipes o quipes

kibbehs

YIELD 12 kipes   **PREP TIME** 30 minutes, plus 9 hours' rest and chill time   **COOK TIME** 20 minutes

The Dominican version of Lebanese kibbeh is one of the most common foods influenced by Middle East immigrants who came to the Dominican Republic starting in the late nineteenth century. This popular appetizer is made with seasoned bulgur wheat and is filled with cooked ground beef for a crispy bite that's full of flavor. You can often find kipes sold by street vendors around the island, and no picadera is ever complete without this tasty dish.

kipes

1 cup (140 g) bulgur wheat

8 to 10 mint leaves

1 small onion, cut in half

1 pound (454 g) ground beef

1½ teaspoons adobo seasoning

1¼ teaspoons ground black pepper

1 recipe Ground Beef Filling
(page 47)

3 to 4 cups (720 to 960 ml)
vegetable oil, for deep-frying

mayo-ketchup sauce
(optional)

3 tablespoons mayonnaise

1½ tablespoons ketchup

½ teaspoon garlic powder

1 **To make the kipes:** In a medium bowl, add about 2 cups (480 ml) of water to the bulgur (or enough to cover it). Cover the bowl with plastic wrap and let soak for at least 5 hours, or overnight.

2 Drain the bulgur. Make sure to remove all the water from the bulgur, so squeeze it with your hands or a clean sackcloth towel or cheesecloth if you need to.

3 In a food processor or blender, pulse the mint and onion for about 30 seconds, or until finely chopped.

4 In a large bowl, mix the 1 pound (454 g) ground beef, onion-mint mixture, adobo, and pepper until combined. Transfer to the food processor or blender and add the bulgur. Process until a uniform mixture is achieved.

5 Place 3 tablespoons of the bulgur mixture on the palm of one of your hands and flatten it with the palm of the other hand. Place about 1 tablespoon of the ground beef filling in the center and roll the mixture around the filling to close it. Make sure that it is completely sealed, using your hands to roll and shape it. Place the kipe in a glass baking dish or on a baking sheet lined with parchment paper. Repeat with the remaining bulgur mixture and ground beef. Cover the baking dish or sheet with plastic wrap and refrigerate for at least 4 hours.

6 In a medium pot, heat enough oil to cover the kipes over medium-high heat. Once the oil is hot, deep-fry the kipes, one or two at a time, turning them occasionally, for 6 to 8 minutes, or until dark brown on the outside. (If the inside of a kipe has any pink parts, it's not fully cooked and needs to fry a bit longer.)

7 Transfer to a plate lined with paper towels to remove excess oil.

8 **To make the mayo-ketchup sauce (if using):** In a small bowl, mix the mayonnaise, ketchup, and garlic powder until well combined.

9 Serve warm with the mayo-ketchup sauce (if using) on the side.

note

Kipe recipes can vary depending on the person preparing them. This delicious version is from my sister, Ibly.

note

If using a glass baking dish, the pan de yuca will bake faster. Start checking for doneness after 30 minutes.

pan de yuca

cassava cake

YIELD 8 servings   PREP TIME 15 minutes   COOK TIME 45 minutes

Unlike Pan de Maíz (page 173) and Pan de Batata (page 174), this cassava cake is not sweet; it is on the savory side with just a slight hint of sweetness. Nevertheless, it is enjoyed in the same fashion as the other two, commonly as an afternoon snack with a cup of coffee.

1 tablespoon unsalted butter, melted and cooled, plus more for greasing (or use cooking spray)

2 pounds (907 g) frozen grated cassava (yuca), thawed

2 large eggs

1 teaspoon anise seed

1 teaspoon salt

2 tablespoons granulated sugar

½ cup (120 ml) evaporated milk

1. Preheat the oven to 350°F (175°C; gas mark 4).

2. Grease an 8 x 4-inch (20 x 10 cm) loaf pan with butter or cooking spray.

3. Squeeze the cassava with a clean sackcloth towel or cheesecloth to remove excess liquid.

4. Transfer the cassava to a medium bowl and mix in the eggs, anise seed, salt, and sugar until well combined. Stir in the milk and melted butter. Evenly spread the mixture into the prepared pan.

5. Bake for about 45 minutes, or until set and a table knife inserted in the center comes out clean (see Note). Let cool in the pan on a cooling rack for about 15 minutes.

6. To remove from the pan, carefully, run a table knife around the edge of the pan. Invert a serving plate over the loaf pan, hold tightly, and quickly turn over. Gently shake the pan to release the bread.

7. Serve warm or at room temperature.

yaniqueques
fried crispy johnnycakes

YIELD 20 yaniqueques   **PREP TIME** 30 minutes, plus 30 minutes' rest time   **COOK TIME** 30 minutes

On the beaches of Santo Domingo, most likely Boca Chica, it's not uncommon to see someone walking down the beach calling out "yaniqueque" and selling this disc-like, crunchy, flaky, fried dough from a wide plastic bowl—a delicious snack that is typical street food at its best. The Dominican yaniqueque is believed to have been inspired by the johnnycake, a cornmeal flatbread commonly eaten in the West Indies and Jamaica, although the dishes don't have much in common except the similar sound of their names.

2 cups (250 g) all-purpose flour, plus more for dusting

1 teaspoon salt

1 tablespoon granulated sugar

3 tablespoons corn or vegetable oil, plus 3 to 4 cups (720 to 960 ml) for deep-frying

Coarse salt, for sprinkling (see Note)

1 In a large bowl, mix the flour, salt, and sugar until combined. Add the 3 tablespoons of oil and combine.

2 Slowly pour in ½ cup (120 ml) of water, a little bit at a time, while working the dough with your hands. Continue working the dough for about 5 minutes, or until all ingredients are incorporated and the dough does not stick to your hands.

3 Cover the bowl with a clean kitchen towel and let rest for at least 30 minutes.

4 Spoon about 1 tablespoon of the dough onto your palm and roll it into a ball using your hands.

5 Using a rolling pin, roll the dough ball on a lightly floured surface until it is a very thin and flat circle. (You can use a round cutter that is about 4 inches in diameter to make it a perfect circle if you would like, but this is not necessary.) Cut 2 small slits, about 1 inch (2.5 cm) long and ½ inch (12 mm) apart, in the center of the dough circle using a paring knife. Repeat this step with the remaining dough.

6 In a medium pot, heat enough of the 3 to 4 cups (720 to 960 ml) of oil to cover the yaniqueques over medium heat. Once the oil is hot, deep-fry the yaniqueques, one at a time, for 2 to 3 minutes on each side, or until golden brown.

7 Transfer to a plate lined with paper towels to remove excess oil.

8 Sprinkle the yaniqueques with coarse salt and serve warm.

note

You can also top the yaniqueques with ketchup, as is commonly done on the island, or with cinnamon and sugar for some sweetness.

note

This recipe is made with tropical avocados, which are larger than Mexican avocados. If you would like to use Mexican avocados, use 2 avocados for this recipe.

pan con aguacate
avocado sandwich

YIELD 2 sandwiches   PREP TIME 15 minutes

Creamy, buttery avocado, lightly seasoned with lime juice, salt, and pepper, is sandwiched between crusty pan de agua (a Dominican bread similar to a French baguette) to make the perfect afternoon snack. This Dominican favorite is best enjoyed with a tall glass of Batido de Lechosa (page 182).

pickled red onions (optional)

¼ small red onion, thinly sliced

1 tablespoon extra-virgin olive oil

3 tablespoons apple cider vinegar

Salt and ground black pepper, to taste

pan con aguacate

1 tropical avocado, pitted, peeled, and cubed (see Note)

1 tablespoon fresh lime juice (about 1 lime)

Salt and ground black pepper, to taste

2 panes de agua (or Portuguese bread rolls)

1. To make the pickled red onions (if using): In a small bowl, mix the onion, olive oil, vinegar, and salt and pepper until well combined. Let sit for 5 to 10 minutes, or until the onion starts to turn pink.

2. To make the pan con aguacate: In a medium bowl, mix the avocado, lime juice, and salt and pepper until combined.

3. Slice the bread rolls in half.

4. To assemble the sandwiches, spread the avocado mixture over the bottom halves of the rolls, add the pickled red onions (if using), and top with the top halves of the rolls.

5. Serve immediately.

chimichurri (chimi) burger

YIELD **6 sandwiches**   PREP TIME **15 minutes**   COOK TIME **20 minutes**

"El Chimi" is the quintessential Dominican street food, typically sold by vendors late at night. The burger is made with a simply seasoned beef patty topped with slightly cooked cabbage, onions, tomato, and a yummy mayo-ketchup sauce, and sandwiched in a bun of pan de agua (a Dominican bread similar to a French baguette). The beauty of this burger is that no two recipes ever taste the same. There's an art to cooking this dish, and every restaurant (or food truck) you visit has its own unique way of making it, although the structure of the recipe is always the same. The delicious burger is usually enjoyed with a really cold beer or a glass of Jugo de Chinola (page 188).

2 small red onions, 1 cut in half and 1 sliced, divided

½ medium bell pepper, cut in half

2 cloves garlic

1 teaspoon dried Dominican oregano

½ teaspoon adobo seasoning

1 teaspoon salt, plus more for seasoning

¼ teaspoon ground black pepper

1½ pounds (680 g) lean ground beef

2 tablespoons soy sauce, divided

3 cups (285 g) finely shredded cabbage

3 tablespoons mayonnaise

1½ tablespoons ketchup

½ teaspoon garlic powder

6 panes de agua (or Portuguese bread rolls, kaiser rolls, or hamburger buns)

2 large tomatoes, sliced

1. In a food processor or blender, pulse the halved onion, the bell pepper, garlic, oregano, adobo, salt, and black pepper into a coarse paste.

2. Place the ground beef in a large bowl and add the paste-like mixture and 1 tablespoon of the soy sauce. Mix until well combined.

3. Divide the meat mixture into 6 portions of about ¼ pound (113 g) each. Using your hands, shape each portion into a ball and then flatten slightly to make it into a patty.

4. Heat a stovetop grill or a large nonstick skillet over medium-high heat. Cook the meat patties for 4 to 5 minutes on each side, or your desired doneness. You may need to cook them in batches. Remove from the pan.

5. Add the cabbage to the same pan. Stir in the remaining 1 tablespoon soy sauce and sprinkle with a pinch of salt. Cook the cabbage, stirring occasionally, for about 2 minutes, or until slightly wilted. Remove from the heat.

6. In a small bowl, mix the mayonnaise, ketchup, and garlic powder until well combined.

7. Slice the bread rolls in half and toast on the grill pan or in the skillet for about 1 minute per side, until crisp.

8. To assemble the burgers, place a meat patty on the bottom halves of the rolls and top with the tomato slices, sliced onions, cabbage, mayo-ketchup sauce, and the top halves of the rolls.

9. Serve immediately.

note

If cooking the patties
on an outdoor grill, I
recommend that you cover
the grill rack with aluminum
foil before placing the
patties; otherwise,
the patties could
stick to the grill.

sandwich de pierna

pulled pork sandwich

YIELD 4 sandwiches   **PREP TIME** 10 minutes   **COOK TIME** 15 minutes

With its airy texture and crusty exterior, a lightly toasted pan de agua (a Dominican bread similar to a French baguette) is the perfect vehicle for leftover Puerco Asado (page 130), smothered in onions, cubanelle pepper slices, and soy sauce. Top the sandwich with slightly cooked cabbage, tomato, and mayo-ketchup sauce for the finishing touch.

½ cup (60 g) sliced red onion

2 tablespoons apple cider vinegar

Salt and ground black pepper, to taste

1 tablespoon vegetable oil

2 cups (190 g) finely shredded cabbage

4 tablespoons soy sauce, divided

3 cups (750 g) Puerco Asado (page 130), shredded and trimmed of any excess fat

½ cup (45 g) sliced cubanelle pepper

2 tablespoons butter

4 panes de agua (or Portuguese bread rolls or Italian rolls) (see Note)

3 tablespoons mayonnaise

1½ tablespoons ketchup

½ teaspoon garlic powder

2 tomatoes, sliced

1. In a small bowl, combine the onion and vinegar. Season with salt and pepper and mix until combined. Set aside.

2. Heat the oil in a large skillet over medium-high heat. Add the cabbage and cook, stirring occasionally, for about 1 minute. Add 2 tablespoons of the soy sauce and season with salt and pepper. Stir to combine and let cook for about 2 more minutes, stirring occasionally. Remove from the pan and set aside.

3. Add the puerco asado to the same pan and cook and stir for 2 minutes. Add the onion-vinegar mixture, cubanelle pepper slices, and the remaining 2 tablespoons soy sauce to the pan. Cook, stirring occasionally, for about 10 minutes, or until the onion is soft and translucent. Remove from the heat.

4. In a separate large skillet, melt the butter over medium-high heat. Slice the bread rolls in half and toast each half, cut sides down, for 1 to 2 minutes, or until slightly golden brown.

5. In a small bowl, mix the mayonnaise, ketchup, and garlic powder, until well combined.

6. To assemble the sandwiches, spread about a tablespoon of mayo-ketchup sauce on the bottom half of each roll, then layer with the pulled pork, tomato, and cabbage, in that order. Top with more mayo-ketchup sauce to taste and the top halves of the rolls.

7. Serve immediately.

shredded chicken filling

YIELD 3 cups (450 g)   PREP TIME 10 minutes   COOK TIME 15 minutes

This recipe can be used to fill Pastelitos (page 29) and Chulitos (page 30),
and can even be used as a layer in Pastelón de Plátano Maduro (page 113).

1 tablespoon vegetable oil

½ cup (75 g) chopped green bell pepper

¼ cup (35 g) chopped red onion

1 clove garlic, minced

1 teaspoon granulated chicken bouillon

½ cup (120 ml) tomato sauce

3 cups (405 g) shredded rotisserie chicken

1 tablespoon chopped fresh cilantro

Salt and ground black pepper, to taste

1 In a medium skillet, heat the oil over medium-high heat. Add the bell pepper, onion, garlic, and chicken bouillon and cook and stir for 5 to 7 minutes, or until the onion is translucent.

2 Stir in the tomato sauce and let cook for about 2 minutes, then add ¼ cup (60 ml) of water.

3 Add the chicken and stir to combine. Let cook for an additional 5 minutes, or until most of the liquid has evaporated. Stir in the cilantro and season with salt and pepper.

4 Let cool to room temperature before using as a filling.

ground beef filling

YIELD 2 cups (300 g)　　PREP TIME 10 minutes　　COOK TIME 25 minutes

Ground beef is a popular filling for Kipes (page 34),
Pastelitos (page 29), and Chulitos (page 30).

½ small red onion, in 1 piece

½ cubanelle pepper, in 1 piece

1 clove garlic

1 tablespoon chopped
fresh cilantro

½ pound (227 g) lean ground beef

½ teaspoon adobo seasoning

½ teaspoon dried Dominican oregano

½ teaspoon ground black pepper

2 tablespoons vegetable oil

¼ cup (60 ml) tomato sauce

¼ cup (40 g) pitted whole or
sliced green olives or
alcaparrado (optional)

¼ cup (35 g) raisins (optional)

1　In a food processor or blender, pulse the onion, cubanelle pepper, garlic, and cilantro for 30 to 60 seconds, or until finely chopped.

2　In a medium bowl, mix the chopped vegetables with the ground beef until combined. Stir in the adobo, oregano, and black pepper and combine well.

3　In a medium skillet, heat the oil over medium-high heat. Add the meat mixture and cook for 5 to 10 minutes, or until browned.

4　Stir in the tomato sauce, olives (if using), raisins (if using), and ½ cup (120 ml) of water. Let simmer over medium heat for 10 to 15 minutes, or until the liquid has evaporated.

5　Remove from the heat and let cool to room temperature before using as a filling.

salads & sides

No meal is complete without a delectable side dish to inspire your appetite and brighten your plate. This chapter is filled with traditional sides, such as arroz blanco, habichuelas guisadas, and moro de habichuelas rojas, along with some favorites, such as plátanos fritos and yuca con cebolla. You'll get a taste of Middle Eastern flavors with arroz con fideos and find instructions on how to prepare the perfect concón. Salads are typically served as an additional side dish to add color and freshness to meals. There's nothing like an ensalada de aguacate to light up a meal or an ensalada rusa to complete your holiday feast.

note

You can also cut the avocado into thin or thick slices and arrange the slices on a large plate or platter before dressing them.

ensalada de aguacate
avocado salad

YIELD 4 servings   PREP TIME 15 minutes

It's rare to see a Dominican meal served without sliced avocado on the side, making it feel as though the tropical fruit has become an integral part of the cuisine. The simple onion vinaigrette in this salad elevates the buttery main ingredient, making it the perfect complement for any meal. It also works really well to make Pan con Aguacate (page 41).

¼ small red onion, thinly sliced

1 tablespoon extra-virgin olive oil

3 tablespoons apple cider vinegar

Salt and ground black pepper, to taste

2 tropical avocados, peeled, pitted, and cubed (see Note)

1 teaspoon roughly chopped fresh parsley

1 In a small bowl, mix the onion, olive oil, vinegar, and salt and pepper until well combined. Let sit for 5 to 10 minutes, or until the onion starts to turn pink.

2 Add the avocado to a serving bowl, top with the onion, and coat with the dressing. Sprinkle with the parsley before serving.

3 Serve immediately.

ensalada de hojas
o ensalada verde
garden salad

YIELD **6 servings**   PREP TIME **20 minutes**

Most meals in the Dominican Republic are served with a fresh salad. This garden salad is easy to put together with green leaf lettuce, finely shredded cabbage, a tomato, and a cucumber. The dressing is a simple vinaigrette made with olive oil, apple cider vinegar, salt, and pepper.

¾ pound (340 g) green leaf lettuce, rinsed (about 1 medium head lettuce)

3 cups (285 g) finely shredded cabbage, rinsed

1 medium tomato, sliced

1 large cucumber, sliced

¼ cup (60 ml) apple cider vinegar

2 tablespoons extra-virgin olive oil

½ teaspoon salt

⅛ teaspoon ground black pepper

1 Arrange the lettuce around the outer edge of a platter, then place the cabbage in the center. Layer the tomato and cucumber on the lettuce around the cabbage.

2 In a small bowl, whisk together the vinegar, olive oil, salt, and black pepper for about 30 seconds, or until well combined.

3 Serve the vinaigrette on the side or drizzle it over the salad as desired.

4 Serve immediately.

note

You can add other ingredients to this salad, such as thinly sliced onions and radish, grated carrots, and boiled and sliced beets.

note

Cook the chayote with the skin on, let it cool, and then peel. This makes it easier to remove the skin.

ensalada de tayota, zanahoria y huevos
chayote, carrot, and egg salad

YIELD **2 servings**   PREP TIME **15 minutes**   COOK TIME **15 minutes**

My grandma's favorite, this salad consists of just three main ingredients: chayote, carrots, and eggs. They are all boiled and served with a simple onion vinaigrette.

1 large chayote (tayota), cut in quarters

1 large carrot, peeled and cut in half

2 large eggs

½ teaspoon salt, plus more to taste for the dressing

¼ small red onion, thinly sliced

1 tablespoon extra-virgin olive oil

3 tablespoons apple cider vinegar

Ground black pepper, to taste

1. In a medium pot, boil the chayote, carrot, and eggs with the salt over medium-high heat for 10 to 15 minutes, or until the vegetables are fork-tender. Remove from the pot and let cool.

2. Meanwhile, make the dressing. In a small bowl, mix the onion, oil, vinegar, and salt and pepper until well combined. Let sit for 5 to 10 minutes, or until the onion starts to turn pink.

3. Once cooled, peel and slice the chayote, then slice the carrot into rounds (see Note). Peel the eggs and cut them into quarters.

4. On a large plate or platter, nicely arrange the vegetables and eggs. Top with the onion and drizzle with the dressing.

ensalada rusa
potato salad

YIELD 8 servings   PREP TIME 20 minutes   COOK TIME 20 minutes

Almost every country has its own version of potato salad, and this ensalada rusa, also called ensalada de papa and Olivier salad, is quite popular in the Dominican Republic, especially around the holidays. It was popularized by a Russian cook named Lucien Olivier in the 1800s, and it's now known and cooked in households around Europe and throughout Latin America. It's typically prepared two ways: with beets, like here, or without beets, which is known as ensalada mixta, or mixed salad. This salad is traditionally served for holiday dinner with Puerco Asado (page 130) and Moro de Habichuelas Rojas (page 67).

2½ pounds (1.1 kg) russet potatoes, peeled and cut in half

1 pound (454 g) carrots, peeled and cut into 3-inch (7.5 cm) pieces

¾ teaspoon plus pinch salt, divided

6 large eggs

1 cup (125 g) chopped red onion

2 tablespoons apple cider vinegar

Pinch ground black pepper

1 cup (135 g) frozen green peas, thawed

½ cup (140 g) sweet corn kernels, if canned, drain, or if frozen, thaw

1 can (14.5 ounces, or 411 g) sliced beets, cubed (optional) (see Note)

1 cup (210 g) mayonnaise

1 In a large pot, boil the potatoes and the carrots with the ¾ teaspoon salt over medium-high heat for 15 to 20 minutes, or until tender. Remove from the heat, drain the water, and let cool.

2 In a small pot, boil the eggs over medium-high heat for about 10 minutes, or until cooked. Remove from the heat, drain the water, and let cool.

3 Meanwhile, place the onion in a small bowl. Stir in the vinegar and the pinch each of salt and pepper and set aside.

4 Cut the cooled potatoes, carrots, and eggs into cubes and transfer to a large bowl. Add the peas, corn, onion, beets (if using), and mayonnaise. Mix to combine well.

5 Serve immediately or refrigerate until ready to serve.

note

This recipe calls for canned beets, but fresh beets can also be used. Peel them, then boil them with the potatoes and carrots in step 1, until tender. Remove from the pot and let cool before cutting into cubes and mixing into the salad.

note

Let the pasta cool completely before adding the dressing. The mayonnaise will become runny if added while the pasta is still warm.

ensalada de coditos

macaroni salad

YIELD **6 servings**   PREP TIME **10 minutes**   COOK TIME **10 minutes**

For our family gatherings, ensalada de coditos is a must-have side dish. It's deliciously creamy and only requires a few simple ingredients. Every bite is bursting with flavor, and it only takes minutes to prepare. You can also enjoy it with a side of casabe (Dominican cassava bread) or Plátanos Fritos (page 75) for a full meal.

8 ounces (227 g) elbow macaroni pasta

½ cup (105 g) mayonnaise

1 tablespoon apple cider vinegar

¼ teaspoon paprika

Salt and ground black pepper, to taste

½ cup (65 g) frozen peas, thawed

½ cup (55 g) diced red onion

½ cup (75 g) diced red bell pepper

½ pound (227 g) cubed cooked ham

1 Prepare the macaroni according to the package directions. Drain and let cool completely (see Note).

2 In a small bowl, whisk together the mayonnaise, vinegar, paprika, and salt and black pepper until well combined.

3 In a large bowl, combine the cooled pasta with the peas, onion, bell pepper, and ham. Add the mayonnaise dressing and mix until well combined.

arroz blanco
white rice

YIELD **6 servings**   PREP TIME **5 minutes**   COOK TIME **40 minutes**

Rice is an integral part of Dominican cuisine and almost always present at the dinner table. Mastering how to make arroz blanco is crucial, particularly when making concón (see below), which is the Dominican term for the crispy rice at the bottom of the pot. Concón can be made with any rice-based dish, but it's typically prepared with white rice.

2 tablespoons vegetable or corn oil

¼ teaspoon salt

3 cups (555 g) long-grain white rice, rinsed and drained (see Note)

1 In a large pot or caldero, bring the oil, salt, and 3½ cups (840 ml) water to a boil over medium-high heat.

2 Once boiling, add the rice to the pot, reduce the heat to medium, and cook, stirring occasionally, for 10 to 15 minutes, or until the rice has soaked up all the water.

3 Cover the pot with the lid and reduce the heat to low. Let cook for 25 minutes.

4 After 25 minutes, fluff the rice with a large spoon. Cover and continue to cook for 5 more minutes.

5 Serve warm.

how to make the perfect concón

"El dominicano es ñoño con su concón." (Dominicans are fussy about their crispy rice.) Dominicans love crispy rice, also known as concón. When rice is part of a meal, the concón is never missing from the table. When cooking white rice, it is easy to make concón. I recommend using a caldero for best results. Follow steps 3 and 4 of the instructions above, turning the heat slightly higher, to medium-low, and cooking the rice for 10 to 15 minutes longer in step 3, for a cook time of 35 to 40 minutes. When done, transfer the rice to a bowl, then firmly scrape the concón with a spoon to remove it from the caldero. These instructions apply to other rice dishes as well.

note

To keep the rice from turning sticky as it cooks, rinse and drain the rice at least three times to get rid of any surface starch and dirt.

note

I use canned beans, but you can use 2 cups (390 g) of dried beans instead. Simply boil the dried beans for about 1 hour, or until tender, prior to making this recipe, adding 1 cup (240 ml) of cooking liquid or water in step 3.

habichuelas guisadas
stewed red beans

YIELD **4 servings**   PREP TIME **5 minutes**   COOK TIME **20 minutes**

Habichuelas guisadas are the perfect complement to a plate of Arroz Blanco (page 60). These flavorful stewed beans are seasoned with herbs and spices and cooked in a tomato-based sofrito sauce. They are part of La Bandera Dominicana (the Dominican flag), the Dominican Republic's national dish, and are served with Pollo Guisado (page 118) and white rice.

2 cloves garlic

1 tablespoon vegetable oil

¼ medium onion, in 1 piece

¼ medium red bell pepper, in 1 piece

3 fresh culantro leaves (cilantro ancho)

3 sprigs fresh cilantro

½ chicken bouillon tablet

2 tablespoons tomato sauce

1 tablespoon pimiento-stuffed green olives or alcaparrado

1 teaspoon dried Dominican oregano

¼ teaspoon ground black pepper

1 can (15.5 ounces, or 439 g) red, pinto, or Roman beans, with liquid (see Note)

1 tablespoon fresh lime juice (about 1 lime)

Salt, to taste (optional)

1. Lightly press the garlic cloves with the flat part of a chef's knife to break them a bit.

2. In a medium pot, heat the oil over medium-high heat. Add the garlic, onion, bell pepper, culantro, cilantro, bouillon, tomato sauce, olives, oregano, and black pepper. Cook and stir for about 5 minutes, or until the onion starts to soften.

3. Stir in the beans with the liquid and 2 cups (480 ml) of water and bring to a boil over medium-high heat.

4. Reduce the heat to medium and let simmer for about 15 minutes, or until the liquid reduces to three-quarters and starts to thicken a bit.

5. Using a slotted spoon, remove and discard the garlic, onion, bell pepper, culantro, and cilantro from the pot.

6. Stir in the lime juice and season with salt if desired.

7. Serve warm.

gandules con coco
pigeon peas with coconut milk

YIELD 6 servings   **PREP TIME** 10 minutes   **COOK TIME** 1 hour 10 minutes

Gandules con coco, like Habichuelas Guisadas (page 63), is a popular Dominican side dish eaten over rice. Coconut milk enhances the thick and creamy stew with a delicious tropical flavor. The use of coconut milk originated in the Samaná Peninsula, where it is common in both sweet and savory recipes. Serve with Arroz Blanco (page 60) and Pollo Guisado (page 118) or Bacalao Guisado con Papas (page 145).

28 ounces (1¼ cups, or 794 g) frozen pigeon peas (gandules), thawed (see Note)

2½ teaspoons salt, divided

4 cloves garlic

2 medium sweet peppers (ajíes gustosos), cut in half and seeds removed

½ teaspoon dried Dominican oregano

6 ounces (170 g) kabocha squash (auyama), peeled, seeds removed, and cut into 1-inch (2.5 cm) cubes (about ¼ squash)

2 fresh culantro leaves (cilantro ancho)

3 sprigs fresh cilantro

½ medium cubanelle pepper, in 1 piece

½ small red onion, in 1 piece

1 chicken or vegetable bouillon tablet

3 tablespoons fresh bitter orange juice

¼ teaspoon ground black pepper

1 can (13.5 ounces, or 400 ml) unsweetened coconut milk

1. In a medium bowl, place the pigeon peas with 2 teaspoons of the salt. Rub the pigeon peas and salt together for 5 to 10 seconds. Rinse with cold water and drain. (This helps remove the excess starch from the pigeon peas.)

2. In a large pot, boil the pigeon peas with 6½ cups (1.5 L) of water over medium-high heat for about 45 minutes, or until the pigeon peas are tender. Drain most of the cooking liquid from the pot, leaving about 1 cup (240 ml) in the pot with the pigeon peas.

3. While the pigeon peas are cooking, using a mortar and pestle (pilón), crush the garlic, sweet peppers, oregano, and remaining ½ teaspoon salt into a coarse paste. Set aside.

4. Add 2 cups (480 ml) of water to the pot with the pigeon peas and reserved cooking liquid, along with the garlic-pepper paste, squash, culantro, cilantro, cubanelle pepper, onion, bouillon, bitter orange juice, black pepper, and coconut milk. Reduce the heat to medium and cook for about 25 minutes, or until all the vegetables are tender.

5. Using a slotted spoon, remove and discard the culantro, cilantro, onion, and cubanelle pepper.

6. Then, use the slotted spoon to transfer half of the squash to a food processor or blender. Add about ½ cup (120 ml) of liquid from the pot and process until smooth. Pour the mixture into the pot and stir.

7. Let simmer for about 2 more minutes, then remove from the heat.

8. Serve warm.

note

You can also use fresh or canned pigeon peas. If using canned ones, drain them well, add them to a large pot, and then skip to step 3 in the cooking instructions. Also, in step 4, add an additional cup (240 ml) of water.

note

This recipe also works well with black beans. I use canned beans, but you can use 2 cups (390 g) of dried beans instead. Simply boil the dried beans for about 1 hour, or until tender, prior to making this recipe.

moro de habichuelas rojas
rice with beans

YIELD 6 servings   PREP TIME 5 minutes   COOK TIME 40 minutes

Moro de habichuelas is one of the most common dishes in the Dominican Republic, but it is not unique to the island. The dish was brought over by the Spanish during colonial times, and many variations of it can be found in Latin American and Caribbean countries.

1 small red onion, in 1 piece

½ medium green bell pepper, cut in half

2 cloves garlic

1 tablespoon chopped fresh cilantro, plus more for garnishing (optional)

3 tablespoons vegetable oil

1 tablespoon tomato paste

2 chicken bouillon tablets

½ teaspoon powdered annatto (bija)

1 teaspoon dried Dominican oregano

½ teaspoon adobo seasoning

½ teaspoon ground black pepper

1 can (15.5 ounces, or 439 g) red, pinto, or Roman beans, drained (see Note)

3 cups (555 g) long-grain white rice, rinsed and drained

1. For the sofrito, in a food processor or blender, pulse the onion, bell pepper, garlic, and cilantro for about 30 seconds, or until the texture of a coarse paste. Set aside.

2. In a large pot or caldero, heat the oil over medium heat. Add 2 tablespoons of the sofrito, along with the tomato paste, bouillon, annatto, oregano, adobo, and black pepper. Cook and stir for 2 to 3 minutes, until the sofrito starts to release its aroma.

3. Stir in the beans and 4 cups (960 ml) of water and bring to a boil. Once boiling, add the rice. Let simmer for 10 to 15 minutes, or until the rice has soaked up all the water and begins to dry up. Stir the rice occasionally to prevent it from sticking to the bottom of the pot.

4. Cover the pot with the lid, reduce the heat to low, and let cook for 25 more minutes. Then, carefully stir the rice and beans, cover, and cook for an additional 5 minutes.

5. Garnish with cilantro (if using) and serve warm.

moro de gandules con coco
rice, pigeon peas, and coconut milk

YIELD 6 servings   **PREP TIME** 5 minutes   **COOK TIME** 40 minutes

This is another popular rice dish in the Dominican Republic. Similar to arroz con gandules, a dish in which pigeon peas and rice are cooked together, this Dominican recipe has the addition of coconut milk and is a great example of the usage of coconut in Dominican cooking. It is often served as part of the holiday meal, as well as with everyday meals, alongside Pollo Guisado (page 118) and Ensalada de Aguacate (page 51).

4 cloves garlic

½ teaspoon dried Dominican oregano

¼ cup (30 g) diced red onion

½ medium cubanelle pepper, diced

2 tablespoons tomato sauce

2 chicken or vegetable bouillon tablets

2 tablespoons chopped fresh cilantro

½ teaspoon adobo seasoning

½ teaspoon ground black pepper

1 can (15 ounces, or 425 g) pigeon peas (gandules) (see Note)

2 cans (13.5 ounces, or 400 ml, each) unsweetened coconut milk

3½ cups (645 g) long-grain white rice, rinsed and drained

1 Using a mortar and pestle (pilón), crush the garlic and the oregano into a smooth paste.

2 In a large pot or caldero, combine the garlic-oregano paste, onion, cubanelle pepper, tomato sauce, bouillon, cilantro, adobo, black pepper, pigeon peas, coconut milk, and 1 cup (240 ml) of water. Bring to a boil over medium-high heat.

3 Once boiling, add the rice. Let simmer for 10 to 15 minutes, or until the rice has soaked up all the water and begins to dry up. Stir the rice occasionally to prevent it from sticking to the bottom of the pot.

4 Cover the pot with the lid, reduce the heat to low, and let cook for 25 minutes. Then, carefully stir the rice and pigeon peas, cover, and cook for an additional 5 minutes.

5 Serve warm.

note

You can also use frozen or fresh pigeon peas. Be sure to boil them in water until tender before making this recipe.

note

Be careful not to burn the pasta when it cooks in the oil in step 2.

arroz con fideos
rice and fried noodles

YIELD 6 servings   PREP TIME 5 minutes   COOK TIME 40 minutes

---

Like Kipes (page 34), arroz con fideos was brought to the Dominican Republic by a surge of Middle Eastern immigrants in the late nineteenth century and adapted into our cuisine. This dish is a delightful blend of seasoned rice and noodles. Pair it with Pescado en Coco (page 137) or your choice of meat.

3 tablespoons vegetable or corn oil

6 ounces (170 g) angel hair pasta (fideos), lightly crushed

2 chicken or vegetable bouillon tablets

¼ teaspoon adobo seasoning

¼ teaspoon salt

¼ teaspoon ground black pepper

2½ cups (460 g) long-grain white rice, rinsed and drained

1 In a large pot or caldero, heat the oil over medium-high heat.

2 Add the noodles and cook, stirring occasionally, for about 3 minutes, or until a deep golden brown (see Note). Stir in the bouillon, adobo, salt, pepper, and 5 cups (1.2 L) of water and bring to a boil.

3 Once boiling, add the rice and cook, stirring occasionally, for about 7 minutes, or until the rice has soaked up all the water.

4 Cover the pot with the lid, reduce the heat to low, and let cook for 25 minutes.

5 Fluff the rice with a large spoon, cover, and cook for an additional 5 minutes.

6 Serve warm.

yuca con cebolla
boiled cassava with onions

YIELD 4 servings   PREP TIME 10 minutes   COOK TIME 15 minutes

In the Dominican Republic, it's common for people to eat a heavy breakfast before a day of work. Like Mangú (page 101), boiled yuca (cassava) is also a favorite option at the breakfast table. However, that's not to say that this delicious ingredient is reserved just for breakfast; it's also commonly enjoyed as a side dish for lunch or dinner with a serving of Chivo Guisado (page 125) or Arenque con Huevos (page 146).

3 pounds (1.4 kg) fresh cassava (yuca), peeled and cut into 3-inch (7.5 cm) pieces, then each piece halved lengthwise

1¾ teaspoons salt, divided

1 small red onion, sliced

2 tablespoons apple cider vinegar

¼ teaspoon ground black pepper

2 tablespoons olive oil

1 In a large pot, combine the cassava, 1½ teaspoons of the salt, and 6 cups (1.4 L) of water. Bring to a boil and cook over medium heat for 10 to 15 minutes, or until fork-tender. Using a slotted spoon, remove the cassava from the water and set aside.

2 Meanwhile, in a small bowl, combine the onion, vinegar, pepper, and remaining ¼ teaspoon salt. Let sit for about 15 minutes.

3 In a small skillet, heat the olive oil over medium heat. Add the onions and cook, stirring occasionally, for about 1 minute, or until the onion starts to become translucent. Remove from the skillet.

4 Arrange the boiled cassava on a large plate and top with the cooked onions.

5 Serve warm.

note

If making this dish for breakfast, enjoy with fried cheese, Dominican salami, and fried eggs. See Mangú (page 101) for instructions on how to cook these components.

plátanos fritos
fried plantains

Plantains are such an important component of Dominican cuisine that they have become a cultural emblem. Phrases such as "más dominicano que el plátano" (more Dominican than plantains) or "aplatanado" (being plantain-like) are often used to characterize a foreigner who has adopted our country's customs. The people of the Dominican Republic consume 2.4 billion plantains annually, according to a report, which amounts to more than two hundred per person. Here, I show you how to make both yellow (plátanos maduros) and green (tostones) fried plantains. Serve either type, as a side dish with your favorite entrée for a great meal. To learn more about plantains, see pages 15 and 21.

plátanos maduros
fried sweet plantains

YIELD 4 servings	PREP TIME 10 minutes	COOK TIME 10 minutes

1 cup (240 ml) vegetable or canola oil, for frying

2 very ripe sweet (yellow) plantains, peeled and cut into ½-inch (12 mm) slices (see Note)

Salt, to taste (optional)

1 In a medium skillet, heat the oil over medium heat. Once the oil is hot, fry the plantains for 2 to 3 minutes on each side, or until golden brown. Transfer to a plate lined with a paper towel to remove excess oil.

2 Sprinkle the plantains with salt (if using) and serve warm.

note *To make plátanos maduros, you want to use ripe yellow plantains. As the plantain ripens, the skin starts turning black, and the blacker the skin is, the sweeter the plantain.*

continued on following page

continued from previous page

tostones (fritos verdes)
fried green plantains

YIELD **4 servings**   PREP TIME **10 minutes**   COOK TIME **10 minutes**

---

2 cups (480 ml) vegetable or canola oil, for frying

2 large green plantains, peeled and cut into 1-inch (2.5 cm) pieces

Salt, to taste

1   In a medium skillet, heat the oil over medium heat. Once the oil is hot, fry the plantains for 4 to 5 minutes on each side, or until lightly golden. Transfer to a plate lined with a paper towel to remove excess oil. Keep the skillet over the heat.

2   Using the bottom of a bottle, small saucepan, or a tostonera, press down on the plantains to flatten them to about ¼ inch (6 mm) thick (see Note).

3   Return the flattened plantains to the hot oil. Fry for about 2 minutes on each side, or until crisp around the edges. Transfer to a plate lined with a paper towel to remove excess oil.

4   Sprinkle the tostones with salt and serve warm.

note *If the tostones fall apart when flattening them, it is because they did not cook long enough when frying them the first time. If this happens, return the plantain slices to the oil and let them cook a little longer.*

guineítos
savory green bananas

Guineítos are green, unripe bananas that are boiled to make them tender. This savory side dish is a favorite at roadside restaurants and goes well with any meat or fish.

8 green bananas, peeled (see Note)

1¼ teaspoons salt, divided

½ medium red onion, sliced

½ medium red bell pepper, sliced

2 tablespoons apple cider vinegar

⅛ teaspoon ground black pepper

2 tablespoons vegetable or corn oil

1 In a large pot, boil the bananas with plenty of water and 1 teaspoon of the salt over medium-high heat for 25 to 30 minutes, or until tender.

2 Remove the bananas and cut them into 1-inch (2.5 cm) slices.

3 In a medium bowl, mix the onion, bell pepper, vinegar, black pepper, and remaining ¼ teaspoon salt until well combined.

4 In a small skillet, heat the oil over medium heat. Add the onion-pepper mixture and cook and stir for 3 to 5 minutes, or until the onions start to become soft.

5 Add the green bananas to a large bowl, then carefully stir in the onion-pepper mixture.

6 Arrange in a serving bowl or on a platter and serve warm.

note *It's very important to use unripe bananas for this recipe, as ripe bananas are too soft and sweet and won't produce the same end result.*

batatas fritas
fried sweet potatoes

YIELD **6 servings**   PREP TIME **15 minutes**   COOK TIME **15 minutes**

Batatas fritas are a quick and easy side dish or appetizer. They are a popular choice at beachside restaurants in the Dominican Republic, where they are frequently served with Pescado Frito (page 134) or Chicharrón de Pollo (page 126).

1½ cups (360 ml) vegetable oil, for frying

2½ pounds (1.1 kg) Caribbean sweet potatoes (batatas), peeled and cut into ½-inch (6 mm) slices

Salt, to taste

1 In a medium skillet, heat the oil over medium-high heat. Once the oil is hot, fry the sweet potatoes in a single layer for 2 to 3 minutes on each side, or until cooked through and the outside is golden brown and crispy (see Note). You will need to cook them in two or three batches.

2 Sprinkle the potatoes with salt.

3 Serve warm.

note

Do not overcrowd the skillet when frying the sweet potatoes to ensure they all cook evenly and get crispy.

XXXXXXXXXXXXXXXXXXXXXXXXXXXX

soups
&
stews

Soup is not reserved for chilly days in the Dominican Republic. On a Caribbean island where temperatures are almost always above 80°F (27°C), if you waited for the weather to cool down, you would be waiting a long time to enjoy a bowl of soup. This is why it's not rare or surprising to find us whipping up a pot of sancocho, asopao de camarones, or chapea de gandules con coco in the middle of summer. Some meals are just worth enjoying any time of the year, no matter the temperature.

note

You can use fresh or frozen shrimp for this recipe. If using frozen shrimp, make sure that they are fully thawed before cooking.

asopao de camarones
shrimp and rice soup

YIELD 6 servings   **PREP TIME** 15 minutes   **COOK TIME** 45 minutes

On cool, rainy days in Santo Domingo, one can usually hear someone exclaim, "El día está bueno para un asopao" (The day is perfect for rice soup). Asopao is what we call rice soup on the island, and many Dominicans have childhood memories of watching their tías or abuelas cooking up a big pot of this amazing soup on rainy days. This hearty dinner of shrimp and rice is just one way to prepare this soup. Other variations include substituting the shrimp with chicken or smoked pork meat, such as ribs or pork chops. No matter the variations, it is always served with a side of Plátanos Fritos (page 75).

5 cloves garlic

½ teaspoon dried Dominican oregano

½ teaspoon salt

½ teaspoon ground black pepper

½ teaspoon adobo seasoning

¼ teaspoon powdered annatto (bija)

5 tablespoons fresh bitter orange juice, divided

1 pound (454 g) raw jumbo shrimp, cleaned and deveined (see Note)

1 tablespoon vegetable oil

1 tablespoon whole allspice (malagueta)

1 chicken or vegetable bouillon tablet

1 tablespoon whole or sliced pimiento-stuffed green olives

3 tablespoons tomato sauce

1 small onion, cut in quarters

½ medium cubanelle pepper, cut in half

½ plum tomato, chopped

½ rib celery

4 fresh culantro leaves (cilantro ancho)

3 to 5 sprigs fresh cilantro

¾ cup (140 g) long-grain white rice, rinsed and drained

Sliced avocado, for serving

1 Using a mortar and pestle (pilón), crush the garlic, oregano, and salt into a smooth paste.

2 In a large bowl, mix the garlic-oregano paste, black pepper, adobo, annatto, and 2½ tablespoons of the bitter orange juice until combined. Add the shrimp to the bowl and toss until evenly and thoroughly coated.

3 Heat the oil in a large pot over medium heat. Add the shrimp and cook and stir for 5 to 6 minutes, or until the shrimp start to release their liquid. Remove the shrimp from the pot and set aside.

4 Pour 6 cups (1.4 L) of water into the pot and bring to a boil over medium heat. Add the allspice, bouillon, olives, tomato sauce, onion, cubanelle pepper, tomato, celery, culantro, and cilantro and stir to combine.

5 Stir in the rice, reduce the heat to low, and let simmer, stirring occasionally, for 13 to 15 minutes, or until the rice starts to become tender.

6 Stir in 2 cups (480 ml) of water and the remaining 2½ tablespoons bitter orange juice. Add the shrimp back into the pot and let simmer, stirring occasionally, for an additional 15 to 20 minutes, or until the rice is fully cooked and the shrimp has turned pink.

7 Using a slotted spoon, remove and discard the allspice, culantro, cilantro, onion, celery, and cubanelle pepper.

8 Ladle into soup bowls and serve with sliced avocado on the side.

note

You can use a combination of meats, such as pork, beef, and chicken, but remember that they cook at varied times and temperatures, and you will need to remove from the pot as each one becomes tender.

sancocho dominicano
meat and vegetable stew

YIELD 8 servings   PREP TIME 20 minutes   COOK TIME 2 hours

Sancocho is, without a doubt, one of the best, biggest, and most loved dishes in Dominican cuisine. This hearty stew is traditionally made with a variety of root vegetables and meats. It's always made in large quantities and is meant for sharing. Every time I travel back home to the Dominican Republic, my family gathers and we celebrate being together after months, or sometimes years, apart. Sancocho is always the main dish on the menu for our gatherings, and my aunts and cousins are masters at preparing it. There are many variations of this dish and different ingredient combinations that make it unique to each family. I have never tasted two sancochos that are alike. Nonetheless, preparing this dish and sharing it with your guests is an act of pure love that is felt throughout any Dominican gathering.

sofrito

1 medium red onion. cut in quarters

1 medium bell pepper, cut in quarters and seeds removed

4 cloves garlic

¼ cup (10 g) fresh cilantro

stew

1 pound (454 g) pork loin end chops, cut into 3-inch (7.5 cm) pieces (see Note)

1½ pounds (680 g) pork stew cubes

½ pound (227 g) smoked pork neck bones

1½ teaspoons adobo seasoning, divided

¾ teaspoon ground black pepper, divided

1½ teaspoons dried Dominican oregano

1 tablespoon vegetable oil

1 pound (454 g) kabocha squash (auyama), peeled, seeds removed, and cut in half (about ½ squash)

1. **To make the sofrito:** In a food processor or blender, pulse the onion, bell pepper, garlic, and cilantro until finely chopped. Set aside.

2. **To make the stew:** Trim and remove any excess fat from the pork.

3. In a large bowl, mix 1 teaspoon of the adobo, ½ teaspoon of the black pepper, 1 teaspoon of the oregano, and 2 tablespoons of the sofrito until combined. Add the meat to the spice mixture and coat it well.

4. In a 6-quart (6 L) pot or caldero, heat the oil over medium-high heat. Sear the meat until it is browned on all sides. Cover the pot with the lid and reduce the heat to medium. Let the meat cook for 30 to 40 minutes, or until tender and the liquid has evaporated. Be sure to add water as needed while it cooks so that the meat does not burn. Remove the meat from the pot and set aside.

5. Add the squash, corn, plantains, yautía, cassava, carrot, and enough water to fill three-quarters of the pot. (Do not overfill the pot because you will be adding in the meat later.) Bring to a boil over medium-high heat.

continued on following page

continued from previous page

2 ears corn, cut into 1-inch (2.5 cm) pieces

2 green plantains, peeled and cut into 1-inch (2.5 cm) pieces

1 pound (454 g) white yautía, peeled and cut into 1-inch (2.5 cm) pieces

1 pound (454 g) cassava (yuca), peeled and cut into 2-inch (5 cm) pieces, then each piece halved lengthwise

1 large carrot, peeled and sliced into rounds

2 chicken bouillon tablets

1 teaspoon whole allspice (malagueta)

4 fresh culantro leaves (cilantro ancho)

5 sprigs fresh cilantro

5 sprigs fresh thyme

½ teaspoon crushed red pepper

½ teaspoon salt

1 lime, for squeezing

Arroz Blanco (page 60), for serving

Sliced avocado, for serving

6 Stir in the bouillon and allspice. Reduce the heat to medium and let cook for 15 to 20 minutes, or until the squash is tender.

7 Using a slotted spoon, transfer the squash to a food processor or blender. Add ½ cup (120 ml) each of liquid from the pot and cold water and process until smooth. Pour the mixture into the pot and stir.

8 Using cooking twine, tie the culantro, cilantro, and thyme together tightly, then add it to the pot. Let simmer over medium heat for about 20 more minutes.

9 Stir in the remaining ½ teaspoon adobo, ¼ teaspoon black pepper and ½ teaspoon oregano, along with the red pepper flakes and salt. Add the meat back to the pot and let simmer, still over medium heat, for 10 to 20 minutes, or until the vegetables are tender

10 Using a slotted spoon, remove and discard the bundle of herbs and the allspice.

11 Squeeze in the lime juice before ladling into soup bowls. Serve with arroz blanco and sliced avocado on the side.

sopa de mondongo
tripe stew

YIELD 6 servings	**PREP TIME** 10 minutes	**COOK TIME** 2 hours

Mondongo is a Dominican stew-like meal that is quite popular. This delicious dish is not unique to the Dominican Republic; it can also be found in other countries in Latin America and the Caribbean, such as Colombia, Puerto Rico, and Mexico, where it is known as menudo. The tripe is most recognized for its peculiar flavor and spongy texture. Serve with lime wedges, hot sauce, and a side of Arroz Blanco (page 60) or Plátanos Fritos (page 76).

2½ pounds (1.1 kg) clean honeycomb tripe (see Note)

2 tablespoons fresh lime juice (1 to 2 limes)

1½ teaspoons salt, plus more if needed

½ teaspoon ground black pepper

3 tablespoons vegetable oil

1 small onion, diced

5 cloves garlic, minced

½ medium bell pepper, diced

⅓ cup (80 ml) tomato sauce

1 teaspoon powdered annatto (bija)

½ teaspoon red pepper flakes

1 medium carrot, peeled and cubed

1 medium potato, peeled and cubed

1 tablespoon roughly chopped fresh cilantro

1 tablespoon chopped green onion

Arroz Blanco (page 60), for serving

Hot sauce, for serving

Lime wedges, for serving

1. Place the tripe in a large pot with the lime juice, salt, and pepper. Add enough water to cover the tripe and boil over medium heat for about 1½ hours, or until tender. Turn off the heat. Remove the tripe from the pot and cut it into bite-size pieces. Set aside.

2. In a separate large pot, heat the oil over medium-high heat. Add the onion and garlic and cook and stir for about 5 minutes, or until the onion is soft and translucent.

3. Stir in the bell pepper, tomato sauce, annatto, and red pepper flakes and cook for about 1 minute. Add the carrots, potato, and cooked tripe and cook for about 1 minute more.

4. Pour in 5 cups (1.2 L) of water and stir. Cover the pot with the lid and cook, stirring occasionally, for 15 to 20 minutes, or until the carrots and potatoes are tender.

5. Sprinkle in the cilantro and green onion, season with more salt if needed, and stir together.

6. Ladle into soup bowls and serve with arroz blanco, hot sauce, and lime wedges on the side.

sopa de pico y pala
chicken soup

YIELD 6 servings **PREP TIME** 15 minutes **COOK TIME** 55 minutes

As a child, I would visit el vivero (the live poultry market) with my mom. I'd stand behind the counter next to her, holding her hand, as she ordered a couple of pounds of pico y pala, or chicken feet and neck parts, and always making sure to ask for la ñapa, a Dominican word that means "a little bit extra." We'd go home after a quick stop at el mercado (the farmers market) and she'd make a big pot of this delightful and soothing chicken soup that works wonders for a cold.

1 pound (454 g) chicken feet (see Note)

1 pound (454 g) skinless chicken necks (see Note)

1 teaspoon dried Dominican oregano

1 teaspoon salt, plus more if needed

¾ teaspoon ground black pepper

2 tablespoons vegetable oil

½ teaspoon granulated sugar

5 cloves garlic

1 small onion, cut in quarters

½ medium cubanelle pepper, cut in quarters

4 fresh culantro leaves (cilantro ancho)

5 sprigs fresh cilantro

1 rib celery, sliced

¾ pound (340 g) kabocha squash (auyama), peeled, seeds removed, and cut into 2 large pieces

¾ pound (340 g) carrots, peeled and sliced into rounds

½ pound (227 g) russet potatoes, peeled and cubed

1 teaspoon whole allspice (malagueta)

3 chicken bouillon tablets

¼ cup (60 ml) fresh bitter orange juice

3 ounces (85 g) angel hair pasta (fideos)

Arroz Blanco (page 60), for serving

Sliced avocado, for serving

Lime wedges, for serving

1 Trim and remove any excess fat from the chicken feet and necks.

2 Season the chicken with the oregano, salt, and black pepper.

3 In a large pot, heat the oil over medium-high heat. Sprinkle the sugar into the pot and let it caramelize until dark brown (do not stir). Carefully add the chicken to the pot and sear it on all sides. Cover the pot with the lid and cook the chicken, stirring occasionally, for 25 minutes, or until tender. Remove the chicken from the pot and set aside.

4 To the same pot, add the garlic, onion, cubanelle, culantro, cilantro, celery, squash, carrots, potatoes, allspice, bouillon, bitter orange juice, and 10 cups (2.4 L) of water and bring to a boil over medium-high heat. Let the vegetables cook for about 20 minutes, or until slightly tender.

5 Using a slotted spoon, remove and discard the allspice, then transfer the squash, onion, cubanelle pepper, garlic, culantro, and cilantro to a food processor or blender. Add ½ cup (120 ml) of water and process until smooth. Pass the mixture through a strainer into the pot and stir.

6 Stir in the cooked chicken and the pasta and continue to cook over medium-high heat for 8 to 10 minutes, or until the pasta is tender. Season with more salt if needed.

7 Ladle into soup bowls and serve with arroz blanco, sliced avocado, and lime wedges on the side.

note

If you are not a fan of chicken feet and necks, feel free to substitute with chicken breasts, thighs, or legs.

note

In the Dominican Republic, the broth of this soup is typically made only with fish heads. Fish heads are more affordable than the actual fish and widely used to enhance the flavor of the soup at a lower cost.

sopa de pescado
fish soup

YIELD 6 servings   **PREP TIME** 15 minutes   **COOK TIME** 45 minutes

Sopa de cabeza de pescado or sopa levanta muertos are just a couple of the names this soup is also known as in the Dominican Republic. Many people believe that this soup may bring them back to life after a long night out, and it is often regarded as an excellent hangover remedy. The broth is prepared using fish heads to make a rich fish stock and enhance the flavor of the soup.

1¾ pounds (794 g) whole red snapper, gilled, gutted, and scaled (about 3 fish) (see Note)

¾ teaspoon salt, divided, plus more to taste

4 cloves garlic

½ pound (227 g) kabocha squash (auyama), peeled, seeds removed, and cubed

1 medium carrot, peeled and sliced into rounds

½ pound (227 g) russet potatoes, peeled and cubed

½ medium cubanelle or bell pepper, in 1 piece

½ small onion, in 1 piece

1 rib celery

3 fresh culantro leaves (cilantro ancho)

3 sprigs fresh cilantro

1½ vegetable bouillon tablets

½ teaspoon dried Dominican oregano

2 ounces (57 g) angel hair pasta (fideos)

¼ teaspoon ground black pepper, plus more to taste

2 tablespoons fresh bitter orange juice

Sliced avocado, for serving

Lime wedges, for serving

1 Separate the fish heads from the fish, then add the heads and fish to a large pot with 10 cups (2.4 L) of water. Boil over medium-high heat for about 20 minutes, or until the fish is tender. Turn off the heat. Remove the fish from the broth and reserve the broth.

2 Carefully separate the bones from the fish bodies. Sprinkle ¼ teaspoon of the salt on the fish bodies and set aside. Discard the fish bones and heads.

3 Transfer the fish broth to a separate large pot, passing it through a strainer to avoid having any fish bones in the broth.

4 Lightly press the garlic cloves with the flat part of a chef's knife to break them a bit. Add the garlic, squash, carrots, potatoes, cubanelle pepper, onion, celery, culantro, cilantro, bouillon, oregano, pasta, remaining ½ teaspoon salt, and black pepper to the broth and stir to combine. Cook over medium-high heat, uncovered, for 20 to 25 minutes, or until the vegetables are tender.

5 Using a slotted spoon, transfer the garlic, cubanelle pepper, onion, celery, culantro, cilantro, and half of the squash to a food processor or blender and process until smooth. Pour the mixture through a strainer into the pot and stir.

6 Add the cooked fish to the pot and stir to combine. Stir in the bitter orange juice and season with more salt and pepper.

7 Ladle into soup bowls and serve with sliced avocado and lime wedges on the side.

chapea de gandules con coco
legumes, rice, and coconut soup

YIELD 6 servings   **PREP TIME** 15 minutes   **COOK TIME** 55 minutes

Chapea, also known as chambre, is a rice soup that is commonly made with legumes, such as beans or gandules (pigeon peas). In many cases, root vegetables are added, but not always meat, distinguishing this soup from asopao (rice soup). Of course, like many Dominican dishes, there are numerous variations, and some do include meat. Chapea is frequently prepared with coconut milk in the northern towns of Samaná and Nagua, because the ingredient is popular in those parts of the island. This is my mother's version, which pays homage to her childhood in the coastal town of Nagua. Serve with a side of Plátanos Fritos (page 75).

14 ounces (397 g) frozen pigeon peas (gandules), thawed (see Note)

2 teaspoons salt, divided, plus more to taste

1 teaspoon vegetable oil

5 cloves garlic

1 sweet pepper (ajíes gustosos), cut in half and seeds removed

2 cans (13.5 ounces, or 400 ml, each) unsweetened coconut milk

¼ pound (113 g) kabocha squash (auyama), peeled, seeds removed, and in 1 piece

3 sprigs fresh cilantro

3 fresh culantro leaves (cilantro ancho)

½ rib celery

½ medium cubanelle pepper, in 1 piece

½ small red onion, cut in half

2 vegetable bouillon tablets

½ teaspoon dried Dominican oregano

½ teaspoon ground black pepper

¼ cup (60 ml) fresh bitter orange juice

1 cup (185 g) long-grain white rice, rinsed and drained

1 In a medium bowl, place the pigeon peas with 1 teaspoon of the salt. Rub the pigeon peas and salt together for 5 to 10 seconds. Rinse with cold water and drain. (This helps remove the excess starch from the pigeon peas.)

2 In a large pot, heat the oil over medium-high heat. Add the pigeon peas, cover the pot with the lid, and cook, stirring occasionally, for about 5 minutes. Pour 2 cups (480 ml) of water into the pot and stir. Cover about three-quarters of the pot with the lid and let the pigeon peas cook for about 20 minutes, or until tender and the water has evaporated.

3 While the pigeon peas are cooking, using a mortar and pestle (pilón), crush the garlic, sweet pepper, and ½ teaspoon of the salt into a coarse paste. Set aside.

4 When the pigeon peas are tender, add the garlic-pepper paste to the pot, along with the coconut milk, 6 cups (1.4 L) of water, squash, cilantro, culantro, celery, cubanelle pepper, onion, bouillon, oregano, black pepper, and bitter orange juice. Stir to combine and bring to a boil.

5 Once boiling, stir in the rice and continue to cook for about 15 minutes, or until the squash is tender.

6 Using a slotted spoon, transfer the squash to a food processor or blender. Add about ¼ cup (60 ml) of liquid from the pot and blend until smooth. Pour the mixture into the pot and stir. Reduce the heat to medium and continue to cook, stirring occasionally, for 10 to 15 minutes, or until the rice is tender.

7 Using the slotted spoon, remove and discard the herbs, onion, cubanelle pepper, and celery. Season with more salt.

8 Ladle into soup bowls and serve.

note

You can also use fresh or canned pigeon peas to make this recipe. If using canned pigeon peas, be sure to drain them well, add them to a large pot, and then skip to step 3 in the cooking instructions.

note

This recipe was made with black beans, but other types of beans, such as red, pinto, or Roman beans, will work as well.

sancocho de habichuelas
black bean, meat, and vegetable stew

YIELD 6 servings   **PREP TIME** 15 minutes   **COOK TIME** 2 hours

I never met my grandfather; he passed away when my mother was six months pregnant with me and suffering from several pregnancy difficulties. I grew up believing he was my guardian angel and the reason I am still alive today. Sancocho de habichuelas was said to be his favorite food, which he would frequently request my grandma to prepare. This stew, like Sancocho Dominicano (page 85), combines meat and vegetables, with the addition of beans. It is traditionally served with a side of Arroz Blanco (page 60) for a complete meal.

8 ounces (227 g) dried black beans (about 1¼ cups) (see Note)

5 cloves garlic

½ teaspoon salt

1 tablespoon vegetable oil

1½ pounds (680 g) smoked pork ribs

1 teaspoon dried Dominican oregano

1 teaspoon adobo seasoning

½ teaspoon ground black pepper

½ pound (227 g) yellow yautía, peeled and cut into 2-inch (5 cm) pieces

¾ pound (340 g) purple or white yautía, peeled and cut into 2-inch (5 cm) pieces

1 green plantain, peeled and cut into 1-inch (2.5 cm) pieces

¾ pound (340 g) kabocha squash (auyama), peeled, cut in half, and seeds removed

½ medium red onion, cut in half

½ medium cubanelle or bell pepper, cut in half

2 fresh culantro leaves (cilantro ancho)

5 sprigs fresh cilantro

1 rib celery

2 chicken bouillon tablets

1 teaspoon whole allspice (malagueta)

¼ cup (60 ml) fresh bitter orange juice

Arroz Blanco (page 60), for serving

Sliced avocado, for serving

1 Add the beans to a large pot with plenty of water. Boil the beans over medium-high heat for about 1 hour, or until they are tender, adding water as needed. Drain the beans and set aside. Reserve the cooking liquid.

2 Using a mortar and pestle (pilón), crush the garlic and salt into a smooth paste. Set aside.

3 In a large pot, heat the oil over medium-high heat. Add the smoked ribs, garlic paste, oregano, adobo, and black pepper and cook for about 10 minutes. Stir in 2 cups (480 ml) of water and cook for about 15 minutes, or until the water has evaporated.

4 Stir in the cooked beans, 2½ cups (600 ml) of the bean cooking liquid (or whatever is left), and 3 cups (720 ml) of water. Let cook, still over medium-high heat, for 5 to 10 minutes, or just until it begins to simmer.

5 Add the yellow and purple yautía, plantain, squash, onion, cubanelle pepper, culantro, cilantro, celery, bouillon, and allspice. Cover with the lid and bring to a boil. Let cook for about 15 minutes, or until the squash is tender.

6 Using a slotted spoon, remove and discard the allspice, then transfer the squash, onion, cubanelle pepper, culantro, cilantro, and celery to a food processor or blender. Add 2 cups (480 ml) of water and process until smooth. Pass the mixture through a strainer into the pot and stir.

7 Stir in the bitter orange juice and continue to cook for 5 to 10 minutes, or until the yautía and plantain are tender.

8 Ladle into soup bowls and serve with arroz blanco and sliced avocado on the side.

main dishes

Dominican food is truly made with soul. A lot of heart and care go into preparing each meal, and this is why a single bite of pollo guisado hitting your taste buds feels like a hug. It's why our family gatherings revolve around empaguetadas and why the holiday festivities center around puerco asado. The recipes in this chapter are all homestyle mains packed with sabores criollos (Creole flavors), including rice, meat, and seafood dishes, and, of course, our beloved mangú con los tres golpes.

note

Make sure to use green (unripe) plantains for this recipe, not yellow (ripe sweet plantains). Green and yellow plantains have different flavors and are not interchangeable.

mangú con los tres golpes
mashed plantains with eggs, salami, and fried cheese

YIELD 4 servings   **PREP TIME** 10 minutes   **COOK TIME** 20 minutes

Mangú is a staple in the Dominican Republic and has always been the ultimate Dominican breakfast. The name of this dish derives from the West African word "mangusi," referring to any mashed vegetable from the earth, and it is one of the many dishes in Dominican cuisine that is influenced by our African heritage. It's typically served with los tres golpes (the three hits)—fried eggs, cheese, and salami—to make a complete meal.

4 green plantains, peeled (see page 21) and cut in half, then each piece halved lengthwise (see Note)

¾ teaspoon plus a pinch salt, divided

2 tablespoons butter, unsalted

½ cup (120 ml) room-temperature water

½ cup (60 g) sliced red onion

1 tablespoon apple cider vinegar

1 tablespoon vegetable oil, plus ½ cup (120 ml) for frying

4 large eggs

8 ounces (227 g) queso de freír, cut into slices

8 ounces (227 g) Dominican salami, cut into slices

1   To a large pot, add the plantains and enough water to cover them, along with ¾ teaspoon of the salt. Boil over medium-high heat for 15 to 20 minutes, or until very tender.

2   Drain the plantains and transfer them to a medium bowl. Mash the plantains with a fork until they are very smooth. (You can also use an immersion blender to make the mangú really smooth.) Stir in the butter and add the room-temperature water in stages as you mash, making sure to add as much water as you need to make it smooth. Keep mashing and mixing until very smooth.

3   In a small bowl, combine the onion, vinegar, and remaining pinch of salt. Let sit for about 5 minutes.

4   In a medium skillet, heat the 1 tablespoon of oil over low heat. Add the onions and cook and stir for 1 to 2 minutes, until warmed through. Remove from the pan and set aside.

5   Add the ½ cup (120 ml) of oil to the skillet and increase the heat to medium. Once the oil is hot, add the eggs and fry for 3 to 5 minutes, or until desired doneness. Transfer to a plate lined with paper towels to remove excess oil. Then, add the cheese to the pan and fry for 2 to 3 minutes on each side, or until golden. Transfer to a plate lined with paper towels. Last, add the salami to the pan and cook for 2 to 4 minutes on each side, or until crisped around the edges. Transfer to a plate lined with paper towels.

6   Garnish the mashed plantains with the onions and serve with the fried eggs, cheese, and salami.

locrio de pollo
chicken and rice

YIELD 6 servings   **PREP TIME** 15 minutes   **COOK TIME** 1 hour 15 minutes

Also known as arroz con pollo, this is one of the most common rice dishes in Latin America and the Caribbean. In the Dominican Republic, locrios (a dish consisting of seasoned rice and some type of meat) are a big part of home cooking. You will find many versions of this dish made with different types of meat and even seafood (see the following recipes). Nonetheless, locrio de pollo is, without a doubt, the most popular of all. Serve with Plátanos Fritos (page 75) and Ensalada Verde (page 52).

5 cloves garlic

2 sweet peppers (ajíes gustosos)

1 teaspoon salt

1 teaspoon dried Dominican oregano

½ teaspoon ground black pepper

2 tablespoons fresh lime juice
(1 to 2 limes)

2 pounds (907 g) bone-in, skinless chicken (legs and thighs)
(see Note)

¼ cup (60 ml) vegetable oil

½ teaspoon granulated sugar

½ small red onion, in 1 piece

½ medium green or red bell pepper, cut in half

3 sprigs fresh cilantro

2 chicken bouillon tablets

1½ tablespoons whole pimiento-stuffed green olives (about 6 olives)

½ cup (120 ml) tomato sauce

3 cups (555 g) long-grain white rice, rinsed and drained

1 Using a mortar and pestle (pilón), crush the garlic, sweet peppers, and salt into a smooth paste.

2 In a large bowl or shallow dish, mix the garlic-pepper paste, oregano, black pepper, and lime juice until well combined. Add the chicken and coat with the seasoning.

3 In a large pot or caldero, heat the oil over medium-high heat. Sprinkle the sugar into the pot and let it carmelize until dark brown (do not stir). Carefully add the chicken to the pot and sear it on all sides until the meat is lightly browned. Continue cooking the chicken, adding a little water as needed, for about 20 minutes, or until the chicken is tender. Remove the chicken from the pot and set aside.

4 To the same pot, add the onion, bell pepper, cilantro, bouillon, olives, tomato sauce, and 4 cups (960 ml) of water and stir to combine. Bring to a boil.

5 Once boiling, stir in the rice and cook for about 10 minutes, or until all the water has evaporated, stirring occasionally to prevent the rice from sticking to the bottom of the pot.

6 Once the water has evaporated, stir in the cooked chicken and cover with the lid. Reduce the heat to medium-low and let cook for 30 minutes. After the 30 minutes, carefully stir the rice and chicken and cover. Continue cooking for an additional 5 to 10 minutes, or until the rice is fully cooked and tender. Remove and discard the cilantro, onion, and bell pepper.

7 Serve warm.

note

You can also use chicken breasts. Just be sure not to overcook them, as they will turn dry and chewy. In step 3, remove them from the pot as soon as they start to become tender, 10 to 15 minutes, then in step 6, add them to the pot after the 30 minutes.

note

If longaniza is not available to you, use spicy Italian sausage instead. It is a different type of sausage, but the dish will be just as flavorful.

locrio de longaniza
rice with dominican sausage

YIELD 6 servings   **PREP TIME** 10 minutes   **COOK TIME** 55 minutes

During a summer vacation with the family in the Dominican Republic, we bought some of the best longaniza (Dominican sausage) I've ever tasted. It was from a small local stand along the side of the road on our way to Santiago from Puerto Plata. The freshly made, long sausage links were displayed dangling from wires for drivers to see as they pass by. We stopped by, bought a few pounds, and took it straight home to make locrio de longaniza for dinner. This one-pot rice dish is a great option for a weeknight dinner and is often served with Ensalada Verde (page 52) or Ensalada de Aguacate (page 51).

3 tablespoons vegetable oil

1 pound (454 g) Dominican sausage (longaniza), cut into 1-inch (2.5 cm) links (see Note)

½ medium green bell pepper, diced

½ small red onion, diced

1 clove garlic, minced

2 tablespoons chopped fresh cilantro

2 chicken bouillon tablets

½ teaspoon adobo seasoning

1 teaspoon dried Dominican oregano

1 teaspoon powdered annatto (bija)

½ teaspoon ground black pepper

¼ cup (60 ml) tomato sauce

¼ cup (40 g) whole pimiento-stuffed green olives or alcaparrado

3 cups (55 g) long-grain white rice, rinsed and drained

1   In a large pot or caldero, heat the oil over medium heat. Cook and stir the sausage for about 10 minutes, or until cooked through and the outside is slightly crispy. Remove from the pot and set aside.

2   Remove excess oil from the pot, leaving about 2 tablespoons. Add the bell pepper, onion, garlic, cilantro, bouillon, adobo, oregano, annatto, black pepper, tomato sauce, and olives. Cook and stir over medium heat for 2 to 3 minutes, or until the onion becomes translucent.

3   Add 4 cups (960 ml) of water and bring to a boil. Once boiling, stir in the rice, cover with the lid, and cook for about 10 minutes, or until the water has evaporated, stirring occasionally to prevent the rice from sticking to the bottom of the pot.

4   Once the water has evaporated, add the cooked sausage back into the pot and stir to combine. Reduce the heat to medium-low, cover, and let cook for 25 minutes. After the 25 minutes, carefully stir the rice and cover. Continue cooking for an additional 5 minutes, or until the rice is fully cooked and tender.

5   Serve warm.

locrio de salami
rice with dominican salami

YIELD 6 servings   **PREP TIME** 10 minutes   **COOK TIME** 45 minutes

Locrio de salami is the first recipe I learned to cook at the young age of sixteen. It was probably the only recipe I knew how to cook until after I got married and was pregnant with my first child. I learned this recipe early in my cooking journey because it was my favorite and I wanted to know how to make it myself. This simple rice dish is cooked with a sofrito-based seasoning and Dominican salami, which is commonly used in the Dominican Republic as an inexpensive source of protein. It's often served with Plátanos Fritos (page 75), Ensalada Verde (page 52), and sliced avocado.

2 tablespoons vegetable oil

½ medium green bell pepper, diced

½ medium red onion, diced

1 clove garlic, minced

2 tablespoons chopped fresh cilantro

¼ cup (40 g) whole pimiento-stuffed green olives or alcaparrado

½ cup (120 ml) tomato sauce

1 chicken bouillon tablet

1 teaspoon adobo seasoning

1 teaspoon dried Dominican oregano

½ teaspoon ground black pepper

1 pound (454 g) Dominican salami, cubed (see Note)

3 cups (555 g) long-grain white rice, rinsed and drained

1 In a large pot or caldero, heat the oil over medium heat. Add the bell pepper, onion, garlic, cilantro, olives, tomato sauce, bouillon, adobo, oregano, and black pepper. Cook and stir for 2 to 3 minutes, until the onion becomes translucent.

2 Add the Dominican salami and cook, stirring occasionally, for an additional 5 minutes.

3 Add 4 cups (960 ml) of water and bring to a boil, still over medium heat. Once boiling, stir in the rice and cook for about 10 minutes, or until the water has evaporated, stirring occasionally to prevent the rice from sticking to the bottom of the pot.

4 Once the water has evaporated, reduce the heat to medium-low. Cover the pot with the lid and let cook for 25 minutes. After the 25 minutes, carefully stir the rice and cover. Continue cooking for an additional 5 minutes, or until the rice is fully cooked and tender.

5 Serve warm.

note

You are most likely to find Dominican salami in a grocery store that carries Hispanic products. If you can't find it in your area, try purchasing it online.

note

Be sure to add the second can of sardines right before covering the rice in step 4. This ensures that there will be some whole sardine pieces when the dish is ready to serve.

locrio de pica pica
rice with spicy sardines

YIELD 6 servings   **PREP TIME** 10 minutes   **COOK TIME** 40 minutes

This version of the Dominican locrio (a dish consisting of seasoned rice and some type of meat) is made with canned sardines in spicy tomato sauce, which add a kick and unique flavor to the popular one-pot dish. Enjoy with Plátanos Fritos (page 75) and Ensalada Verde (page 52).

3 tablespoons vegetable oil

4 cloves garlic, minced

½ medium cubanelle pepper, diced

½ medium red onion, diced

2 tablespoons chopped fresh cilantro

2 chicken or vegetable bouillon tablets

1 teaspoon dried Dominican oregano

½ teaspoon adobo seasoning

½ teaspoon ground black pepper

¼ cup (40 g) whole pimiento-stuffed green olives or alcaparrado

2 cans (5.5 ounces, or 155 g, each) sardines in spicy tomato sauce (pica pica), divided

1 tablespoon fresh lime juice (about 1 lime)

3 cups (555 g) long-grain white rice, rinsed and drained

Lime wedges, for serving

1. In a large pot or caldero, heat the oil over medium heat. Add the garlic, cubanelle pepper, onion, cilantro, bouillon, oregano, adobo, black pepper, and olives. Cook and stir for 2 to 3 minutes, or until the onion becomes translucent.

2. Stir in 1 can of the sardines with its tomato sauce and the lime juice and cook for 5 minutes, stirring occasionally.

3. Add 4 cups (960 ml) of water and bring to a boil, still over medium heat. Once boiling, stir in the rice and cook for about 10 minutes, or until the water has evaporated, stirring occasionally to prevent the rice from sticking to the bottom of the pot.

4. Once the water has evaporated, add the remaining can of sardines with its tomato sauce, gently stir to combine, and cover with the lid (see Note). Reduce the heat to medium-low and let cook for 25 minutes. After the 25 minutes, carefully stir the rice and cover. Continue cooking for an additional 5 minutes, or until the rice is fully cooked and tender.

5. Serve warm with lime wedges on the side.

chofán
dominican fried rice

YIELD 6 servings   **PREP TIME** 10 minutes   **COOK TIME** 20 minutes

One of my favorite things about Dominican food is the variety of dishes in our cuisine that have been influenced by other cultures. Such is the case with chofán, the Dominican version of Chinese fried rice (chow fan). Chinese migration to the Dominican Republic started during the second half of the nineteenth century and continues to this day. Today, more than thirty thousand people of Chinese descent live in the Dominican Republic. The island is also home to Santo Domingo's Barrio Chino, one of only two Chinatowns in the Caribbean. For years, Chinese-owned eateries and upscale Chinese restaurants have been influencing Dominican cuisine, with our own adaptations of their famous pica pollo (fried chicken), Chicharrón de Pollo (page 126), and chofán.

5 tablespoons vegetable oil, divided

2 large eggs

Salt, to taste

1 cup (135 g) cubed cooked ham (see Note)

1 medium carrot, cubed

¼ cup (30 g) chopped red onion

¼ cup (35 g) chopped red bell pepper

½ cup (65 g) frozen green peas, thawed

½ cup (70 g) sweet corn kernels, if canned, drain, or if frozen, thaw

4 cups (800 g) Arroz Blanco (page 60)

5 tablespoons soy sauce

1½ cups (290 g) shredded rotisserie chicken

2 tablespoons chopped green onion, plus more for garnishing

1 In a medium skillet, heat 1 tablespoon of the oil over medium-high heat. Add the eggs, breaking up the yolks and stirring to scramble them. Season with salt and cook for about 3 minutes, or until cooked to desired doneness. Remove from the pan and set aside.

2 In a large wok or skillet, heat the remaining 4 tablespoons oil over medium-high heat. Add the ham and cook for about 4 minutes, or until it turns crispy around the edges. Add the carrots and cook and stir for 2 to 3 minutes.

3 Add the red onion, bell pepper, peas, and corn and cook and stir for 5 minutes, or until the onion begins to cook through and becomes translucent.

4 Add the arroz blanco and mix well until there are no clumps of rice left. Add the soy sauce and stir to combine well.

5 Stir in the chicken, scrambled eggs, and green onion. Cook and stir for about 5 minutes, or until the rice heats through.

6 Garnish with chopped green onion and serve warm.

note

Making chofán is a favorite way to use up leftovers. Often, Dominicans use leftover pork chops instead of ham and cooked chicken from past meals.

note

Traditionally, this pastelón is made with ground beef, but you can easily swap the ground beef for ground turkey, chicken, or lamb.

pastelón de plátano maduro
sweet plantain and beef casserole

YIELD 6 servings   **PREP TIME** 15 minutes   **COOK TIME** 45 minutes

I've always loved the combination of sweet and savory flavors in my meals and so does my family. Layers of ripe sweet plantains, cooked ground beef, and gooey melted cheese make this pastelón de plátano maduro a sweet and savory culinary masterpiece. This dish is often made for family gatherings or a big family dinner, and it's a favorite of adults and children alike. Serve with Ensalada Verde (page 52).

10 ripe sweet (yellow) plantains, peeled and cut in half

1½ teaspoons salt, divided

1 tablespoon unsalted butter, plus more for greasing

2 tablespoons vegetable oil

¼ cup (30 g) chopped red onion

¼ cup (35 g) chopped green bell pepper

1 clove garlic, minced

1 pound (454 g) lean ground beef (see Note)

1 teaspoon dried Dominican oregano

½ teaspoon ground black pepper

½ cup (120 ml) tomato sauce

1 tablespoon sliced pimiento-stuffed green olives

1 cup (110 g) shredded mozzarella cheese

1 cup (115 g) shredded mild cheddar cheese

1 Preheat the oven to 350°F (175°C; gas mark 4). Lightly butter a 8 x 8-inch (20 x 20 cm) baking dish and set aside.

2 To a large pot, add the plantains and enough water to cover them, along with ½ teaspoon of the salt. Boil over medium-high heat for 15 to 20 minutes, or until tender. Drain the plantains and, using a potato masher, mash the plantains until smooth. Add the butter and stir to combine well. Set aside.

3 While the plantains cook, in a large skillet, heat the oil over medium-high heat. Add the onion, bell pepper, and garlic and cook for about 5 minutes, or until the onion becomes translucent.

4 Add the ground beef, breaking it up with a wooden spoon. Stir in the oregano, the remaining 1 teaspoon salt, and the black pepper and cook and stir for about 10 minutes, or until browned.

5 Stir in the tomato sauce, olives, and 1 cup (240 ml) of water. Reduce the heat to medium and let simmer for 10 to 15 minutes, or until all the liquid has evaporated. Remove from the heat.

6 Add half of the mashed plantains to the bottom of the prepared baking dish. Top with the ground beef mixture, using all of it. Sprinkle half of the mozzarella and half of the cheddar on top of the ground beef. Spread the remaining mashed plantains over the cheese, then top with the remaining cheese.

7 Bake, uncovered, for 15 to 20 minutes, until the cheese has completely melted.

8 Serve warm.

espaguetis dominicanos
dominican spaghetti

YIELD 6 servings   **PREP TIME** 10 minutes   **COOK TIME** 20 minutes

---

When we talk about quick and simple recipes, spaghetti is always at the top of the list. The Dominican version of this delicious pasta dish is made with a tomato-based sofrito sauce and Dominican salami for an inexpensive source of protein. The affordable nature of this dish makes it a popular option for large gatherings. Dominicans are even known for making large pots, called empaguetadas, to bring on group trips to the beach, el río (the river), or the lake, a tradition that makes spaghetti the ultimate dish for fun, love, and bonding. Serve with bread, Plátanos Fritos (page 75), and Ensalada Verde (page 52).

1 pound (454 g) spaghetti

1 teaspoon salt

2 tablespoons olive oil

8 ounces (227 g) Dominican salami, cubed (see Note)

½ cup (55 g) chopped red onion

1 green or red bell pepper, sliced

1 clove garlic, minced

1 plum tomato, chopped

2 tablespoons whole pimiento-stuffed green olives or alcaparrado

1 chicken bouillon tablet

½ teaspoon dried Dominican oregano

½ teaspoon ground black pepper

1 cup (240 ml) tomato sauce

1 tablespoon unsalted butter

¼ cup (25 g) grated Parmesan cheese, for topping (optional)

1. In a large pot, cook the spaghetti according to the package directions, adding the salt to the water once it is boiling. Drain the water and set the spaghetti aside.

2. In a large skillet, heat the oil over medium heat. Add the salami and cook and stir until browned.

3. Reduce the heat to medium-low. Add the onion, bell pepper, and garlic and cook, stirring occasionally, for 3 to 4 minutes, until the onion becomes translucent.

4. Stir in the tomato, olives, bouillon, oregano, and black pepper. Cook for about 2 minutes.

5. Stir in the tomato sauce and butter. Let simmer, covered, for 6 to 8 minutes, or until the sauce thickens slightly.

6. Add the cooked spaghetti and stir to combine.

7. Serve hot with the grated Parmesan (if using) on the side.

note

If you don't have Dominican salami, you can substitute it with cooked ham.

note

Other toppings can be used for these tostones rellenos, such as Camarones Guisados (page 141), Shredded Chicken Filling (page 46), and even Ensalada de Aguacate (page 51) for a vegetarian option.

tostones rellenos
stuffed fried green plantains

YIELD 12 tostones rellenos   **PREP TIME** 15 minutes   **COOK TIME** 25 minutes

Tostones rellenos are a tasty and fun way to serve fried plantains. By forming the fried plantains into a cup, you can fill them with your favorite toppings to create a complete meal or great appetizer. In this dish, I top the fried plantain cups with Dominican salami guisado, a traditional and popular Dominican delicacy.

plantain cups

3 cups (720 ml) vegetable oil, for frying

3 green plantains, peeled and cut into 2-inch (5 cm) pieces

Salt, to taste

topping

2 tablespoons vegetable oil

½ small red onion, chopped

½ small green bell pepper, chopped

½ plum tomato, chopped

½ chicken bouillon tablet

½ teaspoon dried Dominican oregano

½ cup (120 ml) tomato sauce

8 ounces (227 g) Dominican salami, cubed

Salt and ground black pepper, to taste

1 tablespoon roughly chopped fresh cilantro, for garnishing (optional)

1 To make the plantain cups: In a medium skillet, heat the 3 cups (720 ml) of oil over medium heat. Fry the plantains, in batches, for 4 to 5 minutes, or until lightly browned on all sides. Remove from the skillet and transfer to a plate lined with paper towels to remove excess oil. Keep the skillet over the heat.

2 Press each plantain piece into the shape of a cup using a deep tostonera. (If you don't have a tostonera, you can press the plantains with a lemon squeezer. Be sure to line the lemon squeezer with plastic wrap before pressing the plantain to keep the cup intact when removing it.)

3 Drop the plantain cups back into the hot oil and fry, in batches, for an additional 2 to 4 minutes, or until golden brown and crispy.

4 Transfer the cups to a plate lined with paper towels to remove excess oil and sprinkle with a little salt.

5 To make the topping: In a large skillet, heat the oil over medium-high heat. Add the onion, bell pepper, and tomato and cook and stir for about 2 minutes, or until the onion becomes translucent.

6 Stir in the bouillon, oregano, and tomato sauce and cook for 3 to 5 minutes. Add the salami, stir to combine, and cook for 5 minutes.

7 Pour in 1 cup (240 ml) of water and let simmer for about 10 minutes, or until reduced to a thick sauce. Season with salt and black pepper.

8 To assemble: Fill the plantain cups with the salami mixture and sprinkle with cilantro to garnish.

9 Serve immediately.

pollo guisado
braised chicken

YIELD 6 servings   **PREP TIME** 15 minutes   **COOK TIME** 35 minutes

If you've ever eaten Dominican food, chances are you've had pollo guisado. This dish is one of
the easiest and most popular dishes in Dominican cooking, and it's one of the main components
in the island's national dish, La Bandera Dominicana (the Dominican flag), which also
consists of Arroz Blanco (page 60) and Habichuelas Guisados (page 63). The chicken is
well seasoned and then braised in a light tomato-based sofrito sauce resulting in a
tender and flavorful meat dish. Serve with Plátanos Fritos (page 75).

6 cloves garlic

½ teaspoon salt

2 tablespoons fresh lime juice
(1 to 2 limes)

1 teaspoon adobo seasoning

1½ teaspoons dried Dominican
oregano

1 teaspoon paprika

1 teaspoon ground black pepper

2 pounds (907 g) bone-in, skinless
chicken (legs and thighs)

2 tablespoons vegetable oil

½ teaspoon light brown sugar

½ plum tomato, chopped

¼ cup (60 ml) tomato sauce

½ small onion, sliced

½ medium green or orange bell
pepper, sliced

1 tablespoon whole or sliced
pimiento-stuffed green olives

1 tablespoon roughly chopped
fresh cilantro

1 Using a mortar and pestle (pilón), crush the garlic and salt into
a smooth paste.

2 In a large bowl or shallow dish, mix the garlic paste, lime juice,
adobo, oregano, paprika, and black pepper until well combined.
Add the chicken and coat with the seasoning.

3 In a large skillet with a lid, heat the oil over medium-high heat (see
Note). Sprinkle the brown sugar in the pan and let it caramelize,
without stirring, for 1 to 2 minutes, or until it turns dark brown.

4 Carefully place the chicken in the skillet in a single layer and sear
on both sides for 2 to 3 minutes, or until golden brown.

5 Pour in ¼ cup (60 ml) of water. Cover the skillet and reduce the
heat to medium. Simmer, stirring occasionally, for 10 to 12 minutes,
or until the liquid has evaporated.

6 Stir in the tomato, tomato sauce and ½ cup (120 ml) of water.
Cover and let simmer for 4 to 5 minutes, or until the tomato starts
to break down.

7 Add the onion, bell pepper, olives, and cilantro and cook, stirring
occasionally, for 5 to 10 minutes, or until the chicken is tender and
the sauce thickens slightly.

8 Serve warm.

note

You will need a large skillet with a lid for this recipe. You can also use a Dutch oven, cast-iron pot, caldero, or any other type of large pot you have on hand.

note

To prepare in a slow cooker, brown the oxtail, then transfer the meat to the slow cooker. Add 1½ cups (360 ml) of water and all the other ingredients and cook for 8 hours on low or 4½ hours on high, until the meat is tender.

rabo encendido
spicy oxtail stew

YIELD 6 servings   **PREP TIME** 15 minutes   **COOK TIME** 1 hour 45 minutes

Rabo encendido literally translates to "tail on fire," and it's one of the few spicy dishes in Dominican cooking. Oxtail is seasoned with a combination of herbs and spices and slowly simmered in a tomato-based sofrito sauce until the meat is so tender, it falls off the bone. I add crushed red pepper for a spicy kick, but any spicy pepper, such as habanero or Scotch bonnet, works well. Adjust the spiciness to your liking or you can leave this ingredient out. Serve this stew with Arroz Blanco (page 60) and sliced avocado.

2 tablespoons vegetable oil

4 pounds (1.8 kg) oxtail, cut into ½-inch (12 mm) pieces

1 teaspoon salt

½ teaspoon ground black pepper

1 teaspoon adobo seasoning

1 teaspoon dried Dominican oregano

¾ teaspoon crushed red pepper

4 cloves garlic, minced

1 medium red onion, sliced

1 medium red or green bell pepper, sliced

1 medium carrot, diced

½ cup (120 ml) tomato sauce

¼ cup (40 g) whole or sliced pimiento-stuffed green olives or alcaparrado

1   In a large pot, heat the oil over medium-high heat. Sprinkle the oxtail with the salt and black pepper, add it to the pot, and sear for 3 to 5 minutes total, or until browned on all sides.

2   Add 3 cups (720 ml) of water and bring to a boil. Reduce the heat to medium-low and let simmer for about 1½ hours, or until tender (see Note). Check the meat occasionally and add more water as needed.

3   When the meat is tender, stir in the adobo, oregano, crushed red pepper, garlic, onion, bell pepper, carrot, tomato sauce, and olives. Let simmer for 10 to 15 minutes, or until all the vegetables are tender and the flavors combine.

4   Serve warm.

bistec encebollado
steak and onions

YIELD 4 servings   PREP TIME 15 minutes   COOK TIME 25 minutes

My mother met my father while working in the cafeteria of a high-end cockfighting club that he was a member of in the Dominican Republic. She stopped working there before I was born, but as a young child, one of my favorite things to do was to visit the club with my dad, with the only intention of eating at the cafeteria. Doña Maria, a tall, middle-aged woman, was one of the best cooks I've ever known. Every time I visited, my father would walk me to the cafeteria as soon as we arrived, sit me at a table, push the door to the kitchen open, and instruct her to serve me whatever I wanted, needlessly, because my order was always the same: "Yo quiero el bistec encebollado con tostones y un quesillo para el postre. Gracias." (I'd like steak and onions with fried plantains and flan for dessert. Thanks.) A sweet smile would appear on Doña Maria's face because she already knew what I would say. "Como lo desees" (As you wish), she would always reply. Serve with Plátanos Fritos (page 75).

½ medium red onion, sliced

1 tablespoon apple cider vinegar

4 cloves garlic

1 teaspoon salt, divided

1 teaspoon dried Dominican oregano

2 tablespoons fresh bitter orange juice

½ teaspoon ground black pepper

1¼ pounds (567 g) round steak, thinly sliced (see Note)

3 tablespoons vegetable oil

Lime wedges, for serving

1. In a medium bowl, mix the onion and vinegar until well combined. Set aside to marinate while you make the steak.

2. Using a mortar and pestle (pilón), crush the garlic and ½ teaspoon of the salt into a smooth paste.

3. In a large bowl or shallow dish, mix the garlic paste, oregano, bitter orange juice, remaining ½ teaspoon salt, and the pepper until well combined. Coat the steak slices in the seasoning.

4. In a large skillet with a lid, heat the oil over medium heat. Cook the meat, covered, stirring occasionally, for about 20 minutes, or until very tender.

5. Stir in the onion and cook for about 2 minutes, or until the onion starts to soften slightly. Cover the skillet, turn off the heat, and let sit for 5 minutes.

6. Serve warm with lime wedges on the side.

note

Be sure to use steak that is thinly sliced (about ¼ inch, or 6 mm, thick) and tenderized; otherwise, use a meat mallet to pound it out yourself before cooking.

note

The rum in this recipe can be substituted with light-colored beer or red wine.

chivo guisado
braised goat

YIELD 8 servings   **PREP TIME** 15 minutes, plus 4 hours' marinating time   **COOK TIME** 1 hour 35 minutes

---

Cooking chivo (goat) is an art in the Dominican Republic. The braised goat meat is well seasoned with a combination of herbs and spices that vary from home to home, and then it's cooked slowly until very tender. The secret to really tasty goat happens when Dominicans add rum, wine, or beer to flavor the meat, a crucial ingredient in the preparation of this national delicacy. Serve with Plátanos Fritos (page 75) and Moro de Habichuelas Rojas (page 67) or Arroz Blanco (page 60).

10 cloves garlic

3 sweet peppers (ajíes gustosos), cut in half and seeds removed

1½ teaspoons salt

2 tablespoons dried Dominican oregano

2 teaspoons adobo seasoning

1 tablespoon ground black pepper

⅓ cup (80 ml) fresh bitter orange juice

½ cup (120 ml) rum (dark or white) (see Note)

5 pounds (2.3 kg) bone-in goat meat, cut into 2-inch (5 cm) cubes

¼ cup (60 ml) vegetable oil

½ cup (120 ml) tomato sauce

½ medium cubanelle or bell pepper, sliced

½ medium red onion, sliced

1 plum tomato, cubed

3 fresh culantro leaves (cilantro ancho), roughly chopped

¼ cup (40 g) whole or sliced pimiento-stuffed green olives or alcaparrado

1 Using a mortar and pestle (pilón), crush the garlic, sweet peppers, salt, and oregano into a coarse paste.

2 In a large bowl, mix the garlic-pepper paste, adobo, black pepper, bitter orange juice, and rum until well combined. Add the meat and coat with the marinade. Cover the bowl and let marinate in the refrigerator for at least 4 hours, or overnight for best results.

3 In a large pot, heat the oil over medium-high heat. Remove the meat from the bowl, reserving the marinade. Sear the meat on all sides, covered with the lid, stirring occasionally, for about 5 minutes, or until it releases all its liquid and is no longer pink. Continue to cook for about 30 minutes, or until all the liquid has evaporated.

4 Stir in the reserved marinade and 3 cups (720 ml) of water. Reduce the heat to medium. Continue cooking, uncovered, stirring occasionally, and adding 1 cup (240 ml) of water at a time as needed, for about 45 minutes, or until the liquid has reduced to about one-quarter and the meat is very tender.

5 Stir in the tomato sauce, cubanelle pepper, onion, tomato, culantro, and olives. Continue cooking for 10 to 15 minutes, or until the onion softens and becomes translucent.

6 Serve warm.

chicharrón de pollo
fried chicken

YIELD 6 servings   **PREP TIME** 15 minutes   **COOK TIME** 25 minutes

This is one of those dishes that is always on the menu of a Dominican restaurant, both on the island and abroad. It's the go-to option for those who don't know what to order because it's a dish that everyone likes. The chicken is seasoned with a combination of dried herbs and spices before it's lightly coated in flour and fried until crispy and golden. Enjoy with a side of Plátanos Fritos (page 75) and a cold beer.

1 tablespoon fresh lime juice (about 1 lime)

5 cloves garlic, mashed

1 teaspoon paprika, divided

1 teaspoon dried Dominican oregano, divided

1 teaspoon salt, divided

½ teaspoon ground black pepper, divided

2 pounds (907 g) chicken thighs, skin on, bone removed (or boneless), and cut into 2-inch (5 cm) pieces

½ cup (65 g) all-purpose flour

2 cups (480 ml) vegetable oil, for deep-frying

Lime wedges, for serving

1 In a large bowl or shallow dish, mix the lime juice, garlic, ½ teaspoon of the paprika, ½ teaspoon of the oregano, ½ teaspoon of the salt, and ¼ teaspoon of the pepper until well combined. Add the chicken and coat with the seasoning.

2 In a medium bowl or clean shallow dish, mix the flour with the remaining ½ teaspoon each of the paprika, oregano, and salt and the remaining ¼ teaspoon pepper until well combined.

3 Coat the chicken lightly with the seasoned flour and shake to remove any excess flour.

4 In a medium pot, heat the oil over medium heat. Deep-fry the chicken, in batches, 3 to 4 minutes per side, or until crispy and deep golden brown. Transfer to a plate lined with paper towels to remove excess oil.

5 Serve warm with lime wedges on the side.

note

*Always season
both the chicken
and the flour for
maximum flavor.*

note

The liver cooks fairly quick. For tender meat, do not cook it longer than 8 to 10 minutes total or it will turn tough and rubbery.

hígado encebollado
liver with onions

YIELD 4 servings   **PREP TIME** 10 minutes   **COOK TIME** 10 minutes

---

Beef liver is high in protein, vitamins, nutrients, and minerals, and beef liver with onions is a delectable recipe that can be prepared in under ten minutes—it's no wonder my mom cooked it often when I was a child. The liver is tender and flavorful, and it pairs well with Arroz Blanco (page 60) and Plátanos Fritos (page 75).

1 teaspoon salt

½ teaspoon ground black pepper

1 teaspoon dried Dominican oregano

3 cloves garlic, minced

1½ pounds (680 g) beef liver, cut into thin slices (about ¼ inch, or 6 mm, thick)

2 tablespoons vegetable oil

¼ medium red bell pepper, sliced

½ small red onion, sliced

1   In a large bowl or shallow dish, mix the salt, black pepper, oregano, and garlic until well combined. Add the liver and coat with the seasoning.

2   In a large skillet, heat the oil over medium heat. Add the liver and sear for 2 to 3 minutes, until browned on both sides.

3   Add the bell pepper and onion and cook and stir for about 5 minutes, or until the onion becomes translucent (see Note).

4   Remove from the heat and serve immediately.

puerco asado o pernil
roasted pork shoulder

YIELD 8 servings   **PREP TIME** 15 minutes, plus 5 hours' marinating time   **COOK TIME** 4 hours

Cooking roasted pork was once reserved for a special occasion, such as Christmas Eve, in the Dominican Republic. A whole pig was cooked over an open fire, and the entire preparation and cooking process took days. Nowadays, roasting pork shoulder in the oven allows you to enjoy this delectable dish all year long. Serve with Moro de Gandules con Coco (page 68) and Ensalada Rusa (page 56) for a traditional holiday dinner.

½ cup (20 g) roughly chopped fresh cilantro

12 cloves garlic

1½ teaspoons dried Dominican oregano

1 teaspoon ground cumin

1½ teaspoons salt

1 teaspoon ground black pepper

1 teaspoon apple cider vinegar

2 tablespoons fresh lime juice (1 to 2 limes)

5 pounds (2.3 kg) bone-in, skin-on pork shoulder

1. In a food processor or blender, pulse the cilantro, garlic, oregano, cumin, salt, pepper, vinegar, and lime juice for about 1 minute, or until well combined.

2. Using a pointy knife, poke holes all over the pork shoulder, about 3 inches (7.5 cm) apart. Rub the seasoning all over the meat, pushing some of it into the small holes. Place the pork shoulder, skin side up, in a roasting pan, cover, and let marinate in the refrigerator for at least 5 hours, or overnight for best results.

3. Remove the meat from the refrigerator and let rest for about 1 hour. This will bring the meat to room temperature and allow it to cook evenly in the oven.

4. Meanwhile, preheat the oven to 350°F (175°C; gas mark 4).

5. Cover the roasting pan with aluminum foil and bake for about 4 hours, or until the pork shoulder reaches a minimum internal temperature of 160°F (71°C). About 1 hour before the meat is done, uncover the pan, and bring the oven temperature up to 450°F (230°C; gas mark 8) so that the skin turns crispy and a deep golden brown. Watch the internal temperature of the meat to avoid overcooking it. If the pork is browning too quickly, turn down the oven temperature and continue cooking until it is done. If the pork is done but the skin is still not crispy, remove from the oven and, using a knife, carefully remove the skin. Place the skin on a baking sheet or pan and bake at 450°F (230°C; gas mark 8) until it is nice and crispy (see Note).

6. Let rest for 15 minutes. Shred the meat using two forks.

7. Serve warm.

note

To prepare in a slow cooker, cook the pork on low for 8 hours or on high for 6 hours. Transfer it to a baking pan, skin side up, and bake at 450°F (230°C) for 15 to 30 minutes, or until the skin is golden brown and crispy.

note

I roast a whole chicken, but you can use 4 pounds (1.8 kg) of chicken legs and thighs instead. Simply bake the chicken legs and thighs at 350°F (175°C), without increasing the temperature, for about 45 minutes.

pollo horneado con wasakaka

roasted chicken with wasakaka sauce

YIELD 6 servings   **PREP TIME** 15 minutes   **COOK TIME** 2 hours

There's a popular restaurant chain in the Dominican Republic that is famous for its roasted chicken. There, the chicken is roasted over a charcoal fire, and their wasakaka sauce—a herb dipping sauce similar to a garlic mojo (a Cuban garlic sauce used for dipping and as a marinade)—is a favorite among Dominicans. As a kid, I remember my uncle driving an hour away to pick up some of the delicious chicken for dinner. The chicken was always juicy and tender, with a delectable flavor. This recipe does not attempt to recreate their recipe because it is not widely known. Nonetheless, the flavor of this chicken is out of this world. Top it with the delicious wasakaka sauce and pair it with Yuca con Cebolla (page 72) or Guineítos (page 77).

roasted chicken

9 cloves garlic

3 sweet peppers (ajíes gustosos), cut in half and seeds removed

½ medium red onion, cut in half

2 teaspoons dried Dominican oregano

2 teaspoons salt

½ teaspoon ground black pepper

3 tablespoons fresh lime juice (1½ to 3 limes)

1 whole chicken (about 4 pounds, or 1.8 kg), with or without skin and giblets removed (see Note)

wasakaka sauce

¼ cup (60 ml) olive oil

½ cup (120 ml) fresh bitter orange juice or lime juice (about 3 bitter oranges or 4 limes)

5 to 6 sweet peppers (ajíes gustosos), cut in half and seeds removed

5 cloves garlic

2 tablespoons chopped fresh cilantro

½ teaspoon dried Dominican oregano

½ teaspoon salt

¼ teaspoon ground black pepper

1 To make the roasted chicken: Preheat the oven to 350°F (175°C; gas mark 4).

2 In a food processor or blender, pulse the 9 garlic cloves, 3 sweet peppers, onion, 2 teaspoons oregano, 2 teaspoons salt, ½ teaspoon black pepper, and lime juice until well combined and the texture of a coarse paste.

3 Place the chicken in a 9 x 13-inch (23 x 33 cm) glass baking dish. Rub the seasoning all over the chicken, including inside and around any crevices.

4 Bake for about 2 hours, or until the chicken reaches an internal temperature of 165°F (74°C) and is a deep golden brown. Fifteen to 20 minutes before the chicken is fully cooked, increase the oven temperature to 450°F (230°C; gas mark 8) so that it turns golden and crispy on the outside.

5 To make the wasakaka sauce: In a food processor or blender, pulse the olive oil, bitter orange juice, 5 to 6 sweet peppers, 5 garlic cloves, cilantro, ½ teaspoon oregano, ½ teaspoon salt, and ¼ teaspoon black pepper for about 1 minute, or until well combined with a uniform texture. Set aside.

6 Serve warm with the wasakaka sauce on the side.

pescado frito
fried fish

YIELD 5 servings   **PREP TIME** 10 minutes   **COOK TIME** 20 minutes

My mother, uncle, a few cousins, and I took a day trip to Playa Najayo, a popular beach in the province of San Cristóbal, west of Santo Domingo, when I was about eight years old. After bathing in the warm, salty waters of the Caribbean, we stopped for lunch at one of the local eateries along the beach. We sat at a table while my mother placed our food order. A tall, slender man in a blue polo shirt and white cap approached us a few minutes later, carrying a large silver tray over his shoulder that he set on our table. My plate was topped with a large, golden-brown fried fish and plátanos fritos. That is where my love of eating fried fish on the beach began. I now go to the beach whenever I visit the island, even if it's just to eat fried fish. Enjoy this dish with a side of Plátanos Fritos (page 75) or Batatas Fritas (page 78).

5 whole snapper fish (about 3 pounds, or 1.4 kg, total), scaled, gilled, and gutted

3 tablespoons fresh lime or lemon juice (about 3 limes or 2 lemons)

1 teaspoon dried Dominican oregano

1½ teaspoons salt

½ teaspoon ground black pepper

2 tablespoons cornstarch

2 tablespoons all-purpose flour

3 to 4 cups (720 to 960 ml) vegetable oil, for deep-frying

Lime wedges, for serving

1 Score the fish diagonally 3 times on both sides.

2 In a small bowl, combine the lime juice, oregano, salt, and pepper.

3 Spoon the seasoning over the fish, making sure it gets into the cuts on both sides, as well as inside the fish.

4 In a shallow dish, mix the cornstarch and flour. Lightly coat each fish in the flour mixture on both sides.

5 In a large skillet, heat enough of the oil to cover most of the fish over medium-high heat. Once the oil is hot, deep-fry the fish, one or two at a time, for about 5 minutes per side, or until golden brown and cooked through (see Note).

6 Transfer the fish to a plate lined with paper towels to remove excess oil.

7 Serve warm with lime wedges on the side.

note

To make pescado frito in the air fryer, spray the bottom of the air fryer tray with nonstick cooking spray and cook the fish at 375°F (190°C) for 20 minutes, flipping it halfway through.

note

*You can also use
red snapper, tilapia,
or any tropical fish
of your choice.*

pescado en coco
fish in coconut sauce

YIELD 4 servings   **PREP TIME** 10 minutes   **COOK TIME** 20 minutes

This recipe comes from the northern peninsula of Samaná, where the use of coconut is prevalent. The fish is simmered in a creamy coconut sauce infused with sofrito flavors. This dish is made in one skillet and is ready in just 30 minutes. Serve with Arroz Blanco (page 60) or Plátanos Fritos (page 75) for a delectable weeknight dinner.

2 pounds (907 g) grouper fillets (about 4 fillets) (see Note)

1 tablespoon fresh lime juice (about 1 lime)

1½ teaspoons dried Dominican oregano, divided

1 teaspoon salt, divided, plus more if needed

¾ teaspoon ground black pepper, divided, plus more if needed

1 can (13.5 ounces, or 400 ml) unsweetened coconut milk

½ cup (60 g) sliced red onion

½ cup (45 g) sliced cubanelle or red bell pepper

2 cloves garlic, minced

½ cup (120 ml) tomato sauce

½ teaspoon powdered annatto (bija)

1 to 2 tablespoons chopped fresh cilantro (optional)

1 Place the fish on a large plate and season both sides with the lime juice and ½ teaspoon each of the oregano, salt, and black pepper. Set aside.

2 In a 12-inch (30 cm) skillet, combine the coconut milk, onion, cubanelle pepper, garlic, and tomato sauce and turn the heat to medium-high. Stir in the remaining 1 teaspoon oregano, remaining ½ teaspoon salt, remaining ¼ teaspoon black pepper, and annatto and bring to a boil.

3 Reduce the heat to medium-low and simmer, stirring occasionally, for about 10 minutes, or until the coconut milk thickens.

4 Add the fish to the skillet in a single layer. Continue to simmer for an additional 10 minutes, or until the fish is cooked through, occasionally spooning liquid over the fish. (Be careful not to stir or move the fish around to keep it from breaking down.) Taste the broth and add more salt and black pepper if needed.

5 Sprinkle with the cilantro (if using) and serve warm.

bacalao con huevos
codfish and eggs

YIELD 4 servings   **PREP TIME** 10 minutes, plus 3 hours' soak time   **COOK TIME** 35 minutes

Bacalao (dried salted cod) is a common ingredient in the Dominican Republic, and it's frequently cooked during Lent, when many people abstain from eating meat. In this recipe, the preserved fish is cooked with onion and bell peppers for flavoring and then enhanced with eggs. The rehydrated, flaked cod provides the only source of salt in this recipe (see Note). Serve with a side of Arroz Blanco (page 60) or Plátanos Fritos (page 75) for a complete meal.

1 pound (454 g) dried salted cod (bacalao), boned

3 tablespoons vegetable oil

1 small red onion, diced

¼ medium red bell pepper, diced

¼ medium green bell pepper, diced

1 teaspoon salt-free complete seasoning (or all-purpose seasoning)

4 large eggs

1   Rinse the cod with cold water, then soak in cold water for 3 to 4 hours. Drain and discard the soaking water.

2   In a large pot, boil the cod in plenty of water for 15 minutes. Drain the water and rinse the cod one more time. (The goal is to remove as much salt from the fish as possible.) Flake the fish with two forks or your hands and set aside.

3   In a large skillet, heat the oil over medium heat. Add the onion and bell peppers and cook for about 5 minutes, stirring occasionally, or until the onion softens.

4   Add the flaked cod and complete seasoning. Stir everything together and cook for about 10 minutes, or until the cod is tender.

5   Stir in the eggs, breaking the yolks and scrambling them slightly as they mix with the cod in the skillet (see Note). Cook and stir for about 5 minutes, or until the eggs are cooked to desired doneness.

6   Serve warm.

note

Before adding the eggs in step 5, taste the bacalao for saltiness. If it is too salty for your taste, add 1 or 2 more eggs to balance out the dish.

note

You can use fresh or frozen shrimp. If using frozen shrimp, be sure to thaw them completely before cooking.

camarones guisados
stewed shrimp

YIELD 6 servings   PREP TIME 10 minutes   COOK TIME 20 minutes

This is one of those dishes that is not exclusive to the Dominican Republic and can be found throughout Latin America, although the preparation and flavors vary from country to country. In the Dominican version, the shrimp is quickly cooked in a simple tomato-based sofrito sauce. I like to add a little bit of crushed red pepper for a mild spicy kick, but this ingredient is optional. Serve with Arroz Blanco (page 60) or Plátanos Fritos (page 75).

2 pounds (907 g) raw jumbo shrimp, cleaned and deveined (see Note)

1 teaspoon dried Dominican oregano

½ teaspoon salt

½ teaspoon ground black pepper

2 tablespoons vegetable oil

½ cup (60 g) sliced red onion

½ cup (45 g) sliced green or red bell pepper

1 clove garlic, minced

½ vegetable bouillon tablet

½ teaspoon crushed red pepper (optional)

½ cup (120 ml) tomato sauce

1 teaspoon fresh lime juice

1 In a large bowl, season the shrimp with the oregano, salt, and black pepper. Set aside.

2 In a large skillet, heat the oil over medium-high heat. Add the onion, bell pepper, garlic, bouillon, and crushed red pepper (if using). Cook and stir for 3 to 5 minutes, or until the onion becomes translucent.

3 Stir in the tomato sauce and cook for 2 minutes. Add the shrimp and stir to combine. Cook, stirring occasionally, for 10 to 15 minutes, or until the shrimp has turned pink with an opaque or white interior.

4 Add the lime juice, stir, and serve warm.

masa de cangrejo guisado
stewed crabmeat

YIELD 6 servings   **PREP TIME** 10 minutes   **COOK TIME** 20 minutes

Dominicans have an affinity for cooking all types of ingredients in a tomato-based sofrito sauce and seafood is no exception. For this dish, juicy lump crabmeat is simmered with onion and peppers until all the flavors come together. This recipe is one that I enjoy most as a filling for Pastelitos (page 29) or as a topping for Tostones Rellenos (page 117). In the Dominican Republic, it's often served for dinner and pairs well with Arroz Blanco (page 60) and Plátanos Fritos (page 75).

2 tablespoons vegetable oil

½ cup (55 g) chopped red onion

½ cup (75 g) chopped green or red bell pepper

1 plum tomato, chopped

½ cup (120 ml) tomato sauce

1 teaspoon dried Dominican oregano

½ teaspoon adobo seasoning

1½ pounds (680 g) lump crabmeat, fresh or canned (see Note)

Salt and ground black pepper, to taste

1 tablespoon fresh lime juice (about 1 lime)

1 In a medium skillet, heat the oil over medium-high heat. Add the onion, bell pepper, and tomato and cook and stir for 3 to 5 minutes, or until the onion becomes translucent.

2 Stir in the tomato sauce, oregano, and adobo and cook for about 5 minutes.

3 Add the crabmeat and stir to combine. Stir in ½ cup (120 ml) of water and cook, stirring occasionally, for 10 to 15 minutes, or until the crabmeat cooks through.

4 Season with salt and black pepper, stir in the lime juice, and remove from the heat.

5 Serve warm.

note

You can use any crabmeat of your choice, but don't use imitation crabmeat because the taste and texture will not be the same.

note

To skip having to boil the fish to remove the salt in step 2, soak it in cold water overnight, making sure to change the water two or three times throughout.

bacalao guisado con papas
stewed codfish with potatoes

YIELD 4 servings　　**PREP TIME** 15 minutes　　**COOK TIME** 35 minutes

---

For this dish, bacalao (dried salted cod), a common Dominican ingredient, is cooked in a rich tomato-based sofrito sauce with onion, bell peppers, and garlic. It becomes a complete dinner with the addition of potatoes, and in the Dominican Republic, it is also eaten with Arroz Blanco (page 60) and sliced avocado.

1 pound (454 g) dried salted cod (bacalao), boned

¾ pound (340 g) potatoes, peeled and diced

2 tablespoons vegetable oil

½ medium red onion, sliced

½ medium green bell pepper, sliced

1 clove garlic, minced

1 plum tomato, diced

1 tablespoon sliced pitted green olives

1 tablespoon roughly chopped fresh cilantro

½ teaspoon dried Dominican oregano

⅛ teaspoon ground black pepper

¾ cup (180 ml) tomato sauce

1. Rinse the cod with cold water, then soak in cold water for 3 to 4 hours (see Note). Drain and discard the soaking water.

2. In a large pot, boil the cod in plenty of water for 15 minutes. Drain the water and rinse the codfish one more time. The goal is to remove as much salt from the fish as possible. Flake the fish with two forks or your hands and set aside.

3. In a separate large pot, boil the potatoes for about 15 minutes, or until tender.

4. In a medium skillet, heat the oil over medium heat. Add the onion, bell pepper, and garlic and cook, stirring occasionally, for 2 to 3 minutes, until the onion starts to soften.

5. Stir in the tomato, olives, cilantro, oregano, and black pepper. Cook for 3 to 4 minutes, or until the tomato begins to release its juices.

6. Stir in the tomato sauce, flaked cod, and ¾ cup (180 ml) of water and bring to a simmer, still over medium heat. Add the potatoes, stir, and continue to cook for 8 to 10 minutes, or until the sauce has thickened.

7. Serve warm.

arenque con huevos
herring and eggs

YIELD 4 servings   **PREP TIME** 20 minutes   **COOK TIME** 15 minutes

---

Arenque (herring) is a preserved fish that made its way to the Dominican shores from Europe and has become an integral part of Dominican cooking. This is one of those ingredients that people either love or dislike; there is no in-between. My mother absolutely loves arenque, preferring it to most proteins, and arenque con huevos is one of her favorite recipes, possibly due to its simplicity. Serve with Yuca con Cebolla (page 72) or Guineítos (page 77).

10 ounces (283 g) smoked salted herring fillets (these come in a bag at the fish market)

5 tablespoons vegetable oil

½ medium red onion, sliced

½ medium red bell pepper, sliced

3 large eggs

1 In a large bowl, soak the herring in cold water for about 30 minutes to rehydrate and remove some of the salt.

2 Drain and discard the water and, using your hands, flake the herring into 1- to 2-inch (2.5 to 5 cm) pieces. Rinse well with water.

3 In a large skillet, heat the oil over medium-high heat. Add the onion, bell pepper, and herring and cook and stir for about 10 minutes, or until the herring releases its liquid and then the liquid evaporates.

4 Stir in the eggs, breaking the yolks and scrambling them slightly as they mix with the herring in the skillet (see Note). Cook and stir for 2 to 3 minutes, or until the eggs are cooked through.

5 Serve warm.

note

Before adding the eggs in step 4, taste the herring for saltiness. If it is too salty for your taste, add 1 or 2 more eggs to balance out the dish.

XXXXXXXXXXXXXXXXXXXXXXXXXXX

desserts

I'm known in my family to be the one with a strong
sweet tooth. I'm convinced that dessert is the best and
most important meal of the day, and no one can tell me
differently. In this chapter, I offer a range of scrumptious
Dominican sweets, from childhood favorites, such as jalao
and conconetes, to a decadent flan de coco and classics,
such as pan de batata and majarete. There's something
here for everyone, children and adults alike.

note

When making this recipe, it's best to mix the ingredients with a food processor or blender so that everything is well combined. You can mix it by hand using a whisk, but it will take a little while longer.

flan de coco o quesillo
coconut flan

YIELD **8 servings**   PREP TIME **10 minutes, plus 4 hours' chill time**   COOK TIME **50 minutes**

Flan is a popular dessert in Spanish and Latin American cultures, including Mexico, Argentina, Cuba, and, of course, the Dominican Republic, where it's known as quesillo. Although some people believe flan and quesillo are two different things, others believe they are the same food with a different name. It's unclear what distinguishes the two sweets, except for the fact that many people approach their ingredient selection and baking procedure differently. This delicate custard recipe uses coconut milk for flavoring and coconut flakes as a garnish.

½ cup (100 g) granulated sugar

5 large eggs

1 can (13.5 ounces, or 400 ml) unsweetened coconut milk

1 can (14 ounces, or 396 g) condensed milk

½ cup (120 ml) evaporated milk

1 teaspoon vanilla extract

¼ cup (20 g) sweetened shredded coconut, for garnishing

1 Preheat the oven to 350°F (175°C; gas mark 4).

2 In a small saucepan, heat the sugar and 1 teaspoon of water over medium heat, stirring constantly, for about 5 minutes, or until melted and golden brown. Pour into an 8-inch (20 cm) round cake pan and, working quickly, swirl the melted sugar around the bottom and sides of the pan to coat.

3 In a food processor or blender, process the eggs, coconut milk, condensed milk, evaporated milk, and vanilla for about 2 minutes, or until well combined (see Note). Pour the mixture into the cake pan.

4 Prepare a baño de maría (water bath) by placing the cake pan in a 9 x 13-inch (23 x 33 cm) baking pan. Fill the outer pan with hot water to about ½ inch (6 mm) in depth. Bake for 45 minutes, or until a table knife inserted in the middle comes out clean.

5 Cool on a wire rack for about 30 minutes, then place the pan in the refrigerator for at least 4 hours.

6 To remove from the pan, place the bottom of the pan in warm water for about 5 minutes. Run a table knife around the edges of the pan. Invert a large round serving plate over the baking pan, hold tightly, and quickly turn over. Gently shake the pan to release.

7 Top with the coconut flakes.

8 Serve immediately or refrigerate until ready to serve.

habichuelas con dulce

YIELD 10 servings   PREP TIME 15 minutes, plus overnight soak time   COOK TIME 3 hours

Habichuelas con dulce is a popular Dominican dessert made most often during Easter, Holy Week, or Lent. Although the Dominican Republic has many dishes that are similar to those found in other Latin countries and cultures, this dish seems to be unique to the island. It's usually prepared in large quantities to share with family and neighbors, and there's not a household on the island where you can't find habichuelas con dulce during Lent. Even in New York City, where there's a strong Dominican community, you can usually find this rich and creamy dessert at local restaurants and being sold by street vendors around the Washington Heights neighborhood.

4 cups (780 g) dried red or pinto beans

1 can (13.5 ounces, or 400 ml) coconut milk

2 cans (12 ounces, or 354 ml, each) evaporated milk

½ teaspoon salt

1½ cups (300 g) granulated sugar

1 pound (454 g) Caribbean sweet potatoes (batatas), peeled and cubed

1 piece fresh ginger (1 inch, or 2.5 cm), peeled

1 teaspoon vanilla extract

2 cinnamon sticks

10 whole cloves

½ cup (75 g) raisins

2 packs (3 ounces, or 85 g, each) round milk crackers

1 Soak the dried beans in water overnight. The next day, discard the water.

2 In a large pot, boil the beans with 6 cups (1.4 L) of water, adding more water as needed, for about 2 hours, or until tender.

3 In a food processor or blender, process the beans with about 7 cups (1.7 L) of water, which should include any leftover water from cooking the beans, for about 30 seconds, or until smooth. Pass the mixture through a strainer into a large bowl and set aside.

4 In a large pot, combine the blended beans, coconut milk, and evaporated milk over medium heat and bring to a boil.

5 Once boiling, stir in the salt, sugar, sweet potatoes, ginger, vanilla, cinnamon sticks, cloves, and raisins. Let simmer, still over medium heat, stirring occasionally, for 45 to 50 minutes, or until the liquid reduces to the consistency of a creamy soup and the sweet potato is tender (see Note). Using a slotted spoon, remove and discard the ginger, cinnamon stickes, and cloves. Remove from the heat and let cool.

6 Serve warm or cold, adding the milk crackers when ready to eat. If eating cold, place in the refrigerator after cooling until it is cold.

note
This dessert can be enjoyed warm or cold. Some people prefer it cold, but I like it both ways. Once the habichuelas con dulce is chilled, it becomes a lot thicker, so keep that in mind when the liquid is reducing in step 5.

dulce de leche cortada

curdled milk fudge

This dessert was made in the days before refrigeration as a way to use spoiled milk. Nowadays, lime juice is used to help the process of curdling the milk. The result is a delicious, candied caramel milk fudge with lime flavor.

4 cups (960 ml) whole milk

1¼ cups (275 g) packed light brown sugar

1 teaspoon vanilla extract

½ teaspoon ground cinnamon

⅛ teaspoon salt

Peel of 1 lime (2 to 3 inches, or 5 to 7.5 cm)

¼ cup (60 ml) fresh lime juice (2 to 4 limes)

1 In a medium saucepan, heat the milk, brown sugar, vanilla, cinnamon, and salt over medium heat. Whisk until the sugar dissolves and bring to a boil (see Note).

2 Once boiling, drop in the lime peel and pour in the lime juice, about 1 teaspoon at a time, around the pot. Do not stir.

3 Let simmer, still over medium heat, without stirring, for about 1 hour, or until the milk curdles and the liquid has reduced completely and turned into a light caramel.

4 Remove and discard the lime peel. Let cool completely, then transfer to an airtight container and refrigerate for at least 2 hours or until ready to serve.

5 Serve in dessert bowls.

note *Place a wooden spoon flat across the top of the saucepan to keep the milk from running over the saucepan when boiling.*

jalea de batata
sweet potato pudding

YIELD 8 servings   **PREP TIME** 15 minutes, plus 2 hours' chill time   **COOK TIME** 30 minutes

Jalea, or dulce, de batata is a dessert that is deeply loved by Dominicans. In almost every town in the Dominican Republic, it is not uncommon to find someone who sells it in plastic jars out of their home. I was given this recipe by my mother-in-law, Gisella Francisco, and the same ratios can be used to make dulce de batata y coco (sweet potato and coconut pudding; see Note). This is a great make-ahead dessert that is perfect as a holiday or housewarming present. Simply bottle it up in a mason jar, chill it, and decorate with gift-wrapping ribbon.

3 pounds (1.4 kg) Caribbean sweet potatoes (batatas), peeled and cubed

3 cinnamon sticks

½ teaspoon salt

5 cups (1.2 L) whole milk

½ teaspoon grated lime peel

1¼ cups (250 g) granulated sugar

1 teaspoon vanilla extract

1 can (12 ounces, or 354 ml) evaporated milk

½ cup (75 g) raisins

1 In a large pot, boil the sweet potatoes in 2 cups (480 ml) of water with the cinnamon sticks and salt for 10 to 15 minutes, or until tender. Remove and discard the cinnamon sticks and drain the sweet potatoes.

2 In a food processor or blender, process the sweet potatoes with the milk until smooth. (You may need to blend in batches.) Pass the mixture through a strainer into a large pot.

3 Add the lime peel, sugar, vanilla, evaporated milk, and raisins to the pot and heat over medium-low heat, stirring constantly to avoid sticking. Let simmer for 10 to 15 minutes, or until thickened to a pudding-like consistency. Remove from the heat.

4 Let the pudding cool to room temperature, stirring occasionally. Transfer to mason jars and refrigerate for at least 2 hours or until ready to serve.

5 Serve in dessert bowls.

note *To make dulce de batata y coco, substitute the evaporated milk with 1½ cups (360 ml) of unsweetened coconut milk and add ½ cup (45 g) of sweetened shredded coconut with the ingredients in step 3.*

note

To save leftovers, store them in an airtight container in the refrigerator for up to 5 days. To reheat, place in a skillet with 1 tablespoon of butter and cook until warmed through.

plátanos al caldero
caramelized ripe plantains

YIELD 4 servings   PREP TIME 5 minutes   COOK TIME 25 minutes

Cooking sweet yellow plantains in butter and then simmering them in a spiced caramel sauce is all it takes to make a spectacular dessert in less than thirty minutes that will wow your guests. This dessert is traditionally served on its own, but topping it with a scoop of vanilla ice cream adds a nice touch.

1 tablespoon unsalted butter

2 ripe sweet (yellow) plantains, peeled and cut in half

¼ cup (55 g) packed light brown sugar

3 cinnamon sticks

8 whole cloves

½ teaspoon vanilla extract

Pinch salt

1. In a medium nonstick skillet with a lid, melt the butter over medium heat. Add the plantains in one layer and cook, turning occasionally, for 5 to 10 minutes, or until browned on all sides.

2. Sprinkle the brown sugar into the pan and add the cinnamon sticks, cloves, vanilla, and pinch of salt. Let cook for about 1 minute, or until the sugar starts to caramelize.

3. Stir in ½ cup (120 ml) of water. Cover the pan with the lid and let simmer, still over medium heat, turning the plantains occasionally, for 10 to 15 minutes, or until the water evaporates and the plantains caramelize. Remove and discard the cinnamon sticks and cloves..

4. Serve warm (see Note).

arroz con leche

rice pudding

YIELD 4 servings   PREP TIME 10 minutes   COOK TIME 35 minutes

Also known as arroz con dulce, this recipe was brought by the Spanish during the colonial period. There are several variations of this dessert throughout Latin America, but the Dominican version is infused with a distinctive blend of spices that is characteristic of Dominican cooking. This recipe is good for four servings but can easily be adjusted to feed more people by doubling the ingredients.

½ cup (90 g) long-grain white rice, rinsed and drained

3 cinnamon sticks

10 whole cloves

½ teaspoon salt

1½ cups (360 ml) evaporated milk

½ cup (100 g) granulated sugar

Peel of 1 lime (1 to 2 inches, or 2.5 to 5 cm)

½ teaspoon vanilla extract

⅛ teaspoon grated or ground nutmeg

¼ cup (35 g) raisins

1 In a large pot, combine the rice, cinnamon sticks, cloves, and salt with 3 cups (720 ml) of water over medium heat. Let simmer for about 20 minutes, or until the rice is tender, stirring occasionally to prevent the rice from sticking to the bottom of the pot. Remove and discard the cinnamon sticks and cloves.

2 Stir in the evaporated milk, sugar, lime peel, vanilla extract, and nutmeg. Bring to a boil over medium-high heat, then add the raisins.

3 Reduce the heat to medium and let simmer for 10 to 15 minutes, or until it reaches a pudding-like consistency. Remove and discard the lime peel. Turn off the heat and cover with the lid to let cool a bit.

4 Serve warm or cold in dessert bowls (see Note).

note

You can serve arroz con leche hot or cold—both ways are delicious! If you plan on serving it cold, let the pudding cool to room temperature, then place it, covered, in the refrigerator for at least 2 hours.

note

Use fresh coconut for this recipe. Prepackaged sweetened shredded coconut is not ideal to use because the recipe benefits from the moisture the fresh coconut provides for a smooth texture.

jalao

YIELD 16 jalao   PREP TIME 30 minutes   COOK TIME 30 minutes

Jalao is a sugar and coconut candy. Its name literally means "pulled" because of its sticky texture when pulled apart. Quick trips to the colmado (corner store) to buy jalao were a daily occurrence back home. Its fresh sweet taste and chewy texture make this amazing candy a childhood favorite.

ingredients

1 cup (220 g) packed light brown sugar

3 cups (300 g) fresh shredded coconut (see Note)

1½ teaspoons fresh ginger, grated

½ teaspoon vanilla extract

⅛ teaspoon salt

supplies

Small cookie scoop (optional)

16 mini cupcake liners

1 In a medium saucepan, heat the sugar over medium-low heat for 10 to 15 minutes, or until the sugar is completely melted and golden brown, stirring the sugar continuously to keep it from burning.

2 Add the coconut and ginger, stirring well to make sure the coconut is completely coated with the caramel.

3 Stir in the vanilla extract and the salt and cook for 10 to 15 minutes, or until the coconut's juices have evaporated. The goal is to get a soft, sticky consistency.

4 Remove from the heat and transfer the coconut mixture to a bowl. Let cool for 15 to 20 minutes.

5 Using a cookie scoop, scoop about 1 tablespoon of the coconut mixture and place it in a mini cupcake liner. (You can also shape the mixture into small balls by rolling it with your hands; this is how it is traditionally done.) Repeat this step with the remaining coconut mixture and cupcake liners.

6 Serve at room temperature.

majarete
corn pudding

YIELD 4 servings   **PREP TIME** 20 minutes   **COOK TIME** 35 minutes

---

Tía Candida was one of the happiest people I've known. Always with a smile on her face, she was a free spirit who never asked for permission and always followed her heart. She was also a great cook. One of her best recipes was majarete, a smooth, creamy pudding-like dessert made with corn and spices. It is typically prepared by grating corn by hand; however, the procedure can be simplified by using a food processor.

4 ears fresh corn, shucked and kernels removed (about 3 cups, or 435 g, fresh corn kernels) (see Note)

1 can (12 ounces, or 354 ml) evaporated milk

1 can (13.5 ounces, or 400 ml) coconut milk

1½ teaspoons cornstarch

½ cup (100 g) granulated sugar

2 cinnamon sticks

¼ teaspoon grated or ground nutmeg

1 teaspoon vanilla extract

1 tablespoon unsalted butter

¼ teaspoon salt

Ground cinnamon, for sprinkling

1 In a food processor or blender, mix the corn kernels with the evaporated milk, coconut milk, and cornstarch for about 2 minutes, or until smooth.

2 Pass the mixture through a strainer two times to separate the liquid from the solids and remove any lumps. Keep the liquid and discard the solids.

3 In a large saucepan, heat the corn mixture over medium heat for about 10 minutes, or until warm.

4 Stir in the sugar, cinnamon sticks, nutmeg, vanilla extract, butter, and salt.

5 Continue to cook, stirring continuously, for 20 to 25 minutes, or until the mixture thickens to a pudding-like consistency. Remove from the heat.

6 Let cool completely. Remove and discard the cinnamon sticks.

7 Pour into small dessert bowls and sprinkle with a little bit of cinnamon. Serve warm or chilled.

note

To neatly remove the corn kernels from the cob, set a small bowl or cup upside down inside a larger bowl. Rest the ear firmly on the small bowl and cut the kernels downward using a knife so that the kernels fall into the bowl.

note

You can store the conconetes in an airtight container and leave them on the kitchen counter for up to 3 days. Many people prefer to eat them the next day rather than freshly baked. I enjoy them all the same.

conconetes

YIELD 18 conconetes   PREP TIME 15 minutes   COOK TIME 20 minutes

Also known as masitas, this is a childhood favorite found at every colmado (corner store) in the Dominican Republic. This recipe was given to me by my aunt Teresa Genao, who learned it from her Tía Consuelo. The recipe was my great-grandma Corina's and has been passed down through four generations. The three of them used to make conconetes to sell by the dozen, back en el campo (the countryside) when my mom was a child. This rustic coconut cookie is perfect to enjoy with a cup of Chocolate Caliente (page 195) or coffee.

3 cups (255 g) sweetened shredded coconut

¾ cup (165 g) packed light brown sugar

½ teaspoon grated fresh ginger

1 teaspoon vanilla extract

½ teaspoon ground cinnamon

¼ teaspoon grated or ground nutmeg

1½ cups (360 ml) evaporated milk

1 teaspoon baking powder

1 teaspoon baking soda

2 cups (250 g) all-purpose flour

1 Preheat the oven to 375°F (190°C; gas mark 5). Line a baking sheet with parchment paper and set aside.

2 In a large bowl, combine the coconut, sugar, ginger, vanilla, cinnamon, and nutmeg. Pour in the evaporated milk and, using a spatula, fold in the ingredients until fully combined.

3 In a medium bowl, stir the baking powder, baking soda, and flour to combine. Fold the flour mixture into the coconut mixture by adding it ½ cup (65 g) at a time until it is just incorporated. Do not overmix.

4 Place 1-tablespoon amounts of the mixture onto the prepared baking sheet, about 2 inches (5 cm) apart.

5 Bake for 20 minutes, or until a toothpick inserted in the center comes out clean and the conconetes are golden brown. Let cool on the baking sheet for 15 minutes.

6 Serve warm or at room temperature (see Note).

bizcocho dominicano
dominican cake

| YIELD 8 servings | PREP TIME 1 hour | COOK TIME 1 hour |

If there's one thing to know about me, it's that I love sweets, cakes, and pastries of all kinds. There's not a restaurant I go to where I leave without trying dessert. Even at home, I always have something sweet after each meal. Of all the cakes I've ever tried, Dominican cake is my absolute favorite. The moist, airy texture and delicious taste make this wonderful cake unique. The frosting is a meringue that we call suspiro, and it is made with egg whites and sugar. Traditionally, Dominican cake is filled with a layer of pineapple jam, creating a unique flavor combination. Other filling options include guayaba (guava) paste and my favorite, dulce de leche.

cake

1 cup (225 g) unsalted butter, softened, plus more for greasing

2 cups (400 g) granulated sugar

6 large eggs

2½ cups (315 g) all-purpose flour

½ cup (65 g) cornstarch

3 teaspoons baking powder

¼ teaspoon salt

¾ cup (180 ml) orange juice (about 3 oranges, if using fresh)

1 teaspoon vanilla extract

1 teaspoon grated orange or lime peel

1 can (13.4 ounces, or 380 g) dulce de leche

meringue

1½ cups (300 g) granulated sugar

½ cup (120 ml) egg whites (about 4 large eggs)

⅛ teaspoon cream of tartar

1 teaspoon white (clear) vanilla extract

½ teaspoon fresh lime juice

supplies

piping bag

1 **To make the cake:** Preheat the oven to 350°F (175°C; gas mark 4). Grease two 8-inch (20 cm) round baking pans with butter. Set aside.

2 In a stand mixer, or using a hand mixer and a large bowl, cream the butter. Add the 2 cups (400 g) sugar slowly and continue beating until the butter turns pale yellow and creamy.

3 Add the eggs, one at a time, beating after each addition until all the eggs are well incorporated.

4 In a medium bowl, sift the flour, cornstarch, baking powder, and salt together.

5 Slowly add the dry ingredients to the wet ingredients, alternating with the orange juice and 1 teaspoon vanilla. Add the orange peel and continue to mix until all ingredients are incorporated. Do not overmix the batter. Transfer the batter to the prepared pans, pouring half of the batter into each one.

6 Bake for 35 to 40 minutes, or until a toothpick inserted in the centers comes out clean. Let cool completely in the pans on a cooling rack before filling and frosting.

7 **To make the meringue:** In a medium saucepan, combine the 1½ cups (300 g) sugar with 1 cup (240 ml) of water over medium heat and bring to a boil. Continue to boil, stirring occasionally, for 20 to 30 minutes, or until it reaches the consistency of syrup. (To know if the syrup is ready, insert a spoon into the syrup and lift it up. If it drips in a consistent stream that looks like a thread, the syrup is ready. It is important that the syrup is at this point or your meringue will not have the right consistency.)

continued on following page

note

It is recommended to serve this cake at room temperature. Refrigerating the cake causes the butter to stiffen, making the texture of the cake seem dry.

continued from previous page

8   Four to 5 minutes before the syrup is ready, begin beating the egg whites and cream of tartar in the clean bowl of a stand mixer using the wire whisk attachment on low speed for about 1 minute, or until the egg whites start to become foamy. Increase the speed to high and continue beating until the egg whites start to form soft peaks.

9   Pour the syrup into the mixer in a slow stream while beating the egg whites on high speed. Continue beating the meringue for 5 to 8 minutes, or until the temperature has cooled a bit and stiff peaks start to form.

10 Mix in the 1 teaspoon white vanilla extract and lime juice. Continue beating the meringue for an additional 5 minutes, or until it has cooled down completely, strong peaks have formed, and the meringue has a glossy shine.

11 **To assemble the cake:** Remove the cakes from the pans by flipping them upside down onto the cooling rack and carefully lifting up the pans. Cut the cake tops to level them and make them even. Place one of the cakes on a cake stand or a flat plate.

12 Fill a piping bag with meringue and cut a ½-inch (12 mm) hole at the tip. Make an outer circle on top of the cake with the meringue. Evenly spread the dulce de leche in the center. Place the second cake on top.

13 Spread the meringue evenly on top and around the sides of the cake. Decorate as desired.

14 Serve at room temperature (see Note on previous page).

pudín de pan
bread pudding

YIELD 8 servings   PREP TIME 15 minutes, plus 4 hours' chill time   COOK TIME 1 hour 5 minutes

---

The use of spices is fundamental in Dominican cooking, including our dessert recipes. This pudín de pan is enhanced with cinnamon and nutmeg, and if you want to be a little extra, sprinkle a bit of ground cloves for a special touch (see Note). This rich and creamy bread pudding can be served hot or cold. It's great on its own with a cup of coffee in the afternoon or served as a dessert with fresh berries or even ice cream.

4 kaiser rolls, broken into 1- to 2-inch (2.5 to 5 cm) pieces

2 cups (480 ml) whole milk

1 can (12 ounces, or 354 ml) evaporated milk

1 can (14 ounces, or 396 g) condensed milk

1 cup (200 g) granulated sugar

¼ cup (55 g) unsalted butter, melted

4 large eggs

1 teaspoon vanilla extract

1 teaspoon ground cinnamon

¼ teaspoon grated or ground nutmeg

1 teaspoon grated lime peel

⅛ teaspoon salt

½ cup (75 g) raisins

1 teaspoon all-purpose flour

1 Preheat the oven to 350°F (175°C; gas mark 4).

2 Put the bread pieces in a large bowl and set aside.

3 In a medium bowl, combine the milk, evaporated milk, and condensed milk. Place the milk mixture in the microwave for 1 minute and heat until just warm.

4 Pour the milk mixture over the bread. Fold the milk and the bread together pressing on the bread to break it down further. (You can use a food processor or blender to blend the bread and milk together until smooth; this will make for a smoother bread pudding with a texture similar to flan.) Set it aside and let rest for about 10 minutes to allow the bread to soak up the milk mixture.

5 In the meantime, prepare the caramel. In a small saucepan, heat the sugar with 1 tablespoon of water over medium heat, stirring constantly, for about 5 minutes, or until melted and golden brown. Pour the caramel into a 9 x 5-inch (23 x 13 cm) loaf pan and, working quickly, swirl the caramel around the bottom and sides of the pan to coat.

6 Fold the melted butter into the bread mixture to combine.

7 In a clean medium bowl, whisk together the eggs, vanilla extract, cinnamon, nutmeg, lime peel, and salt until well combined. Add the egg mixture to the bread mixture and stir until well incorporated.

continued on following page

continued from previous page

8 In a small bowl, coat the raisins with the flour, then add them to the bread mixture. This will prevent the raisins from sinking to the bottom of the pan. Fold to combine.

9 Pour the bread pudding mixture into the loaf pan. Prepare a baño de maría (water bath) by placing the loaf pan in a 9 x 13-inch (23 x 33 cm) baking pan. Fill the outer dish with hot water 1 inch (2.5 cm) in depth.

10 Bake for 1 hour, or until a table knife inserted in the middle comes out clean. Let cool on a wire rack for about 30 minutes. Then, place in the refrigerator for at least 4 hours.

11 To remove from the pan, place the bottom of the pan in warm water for about 5 minutes. Run a table knife around the edges of the pan. Invert a serving plate over the loaf pan, hold tightly, and quickly turn over. Gently shake the pan to release.

12 Serve immediately or refrigerate until ready to serve.

note

For even more spice, add ¼ teaspoon of ground cloves with the cinnamon and nutmeg in step 7.

note

Mix the batter by hand, rather than using a hand or stand mixer so that you do not overwork the batter.

pan de maíz

corn bread

YIELD 8 servings   PREP TIME 15 minutes   COOK TIME 35 minutes

Also known as torta in some parts of the country, this is a traditional corn-bread recipe, not to be confused with arepa, which is a Dominican cornmeal cake that is sweeter in taste and smoother in texture. This recipe is mildly sweet, soft, and buttery with crispy edges. It makes a delicious pairing with your morning or midday coffee.

1 cup (125 g) all-purpose flour

1 cup (180 g) fine yellow cornmeal

¼ cup (55 g) packed light brown sugar

¼ cup (50 g) granulated sugar

1 teaspoon baking powder

½ teaspoon baking soda

¼ teaspoon salt

2 large eggs

½ cup (120 ml) coconut milk

½ cup (120 ml) evaporated milk

½ cup (115 g) unsalted butter, melted

1 Preheat the oven to 400°F (205°C; gas mark 6). Butter an 8 x 4-inch (20 x 10 cm) loaf pan and set aside.

2 In a large bowl, mix the flour, cornmeal, brown sugar, granulated sugar, baking powder, baking soda, and salt until combined.

3 Make a well in the center and add the eggs, coconut milk, and evaporated milk. Whisk everything together to combine.

4 Pour in the melted butter and stir to incorporate into the batter until just combined. Be careful not to overmix the batter (see Note). Transfer the batter to the prepared pan.

5 Bake for 35 to 40 minutes, or until the corn bread starts to brown on top and a toothpick inserted in the center comes out clean.

6 Let cool on a cooling rack for 15 minutes before removing from the pan.

7 Serve warm or at room temperature.

pan de batata
spiced sweet potato cake

YIELD **8 servings**   PREP TIME **20 minutes**   COOK TIME **1 hour 30 minutes**

Pan de batata is an unusual cake in the sense that it does not contain any flour. The main ingredient in this recipe is batata (Caribbean sweet potato), and it is flavored with a combination of spices and fresh ginger. It is traditionally enjoyed as an afternoon snack with a warm cup of coffee.

1½ pounds Caribbean sweet potatoes (batatas), peeled and cut into 1-inch (2.5 cm) cubes

1 can (13.5 ounces, or 400 ml) coconut milk

1 cup (240 ml) evaporated milk

½ cup (45 g) sweetened shredded coconut

¼ cup (55 g) unsweetened butter, melted, plus more for greasing (or use nonstick cooking spray)

1 cup (220 g) packed light brown sugar

1 teaspoon ground cinnamon

½ teaspoon grated or ground nutmeg

¼ teaspoon ground cloves

1½ teaspoons vanilla extract

1 teaspoon grated lime peel

1 tablespoon grated fresh ginger

½ teaspoon salt

1 Preheat the oven to 350°F (175°C; gas mark 4). Grease a 9 x 5-inch (23 x 13 cm) loaf pan with butter or cooking spray.

2 In a food processor or high-powered blender, pulse the sweet potato for about 5 minutes, until grated and smooth. Be sure to stop and scrape down the sides of the bowl a few times to make sure it grates uniformly (see Note). Transfer the sweet potato to a large mixing bowl.

3 Stir in the coconut milk, evaporated milk, shredded coconut, butter, sugar, cinnamon, nutmeg, cloves, vanilla, lime peel, ginger, and salt. Fold with a spatula until well combined. Pour the mixture into the prepared pan.

4 Bake for about 1 hour 30 minutes, or until a table knife inserted in the center comes out clean. Let cool in the pan on a cooling rack for about 30 minutes.

5 To remove from the pan, carefully run a table knife around the edge of the pan. Invert a serving plate over the loaf pan, hold tightly, and quickly turn over. Gently shake the pan to release. Let cool completely before serving.

6 Serve at room temperature.

note

If you don't have a food processor or high-powered blender, you can grate the sweet potato by hand using the side for finely shredding on a box grater.

drinks

Dominican drinks are infused with the warmth of
spices and tropical flavors that are characteristic
of this Caribbean island. Whether it is a comforting,
warm breakfast drink, such as avena caliente, to
start your morning or a fruity, refreshing beverage,
such as morir soñando, to enjoy in the middle
of the day, there's a recipe for you.

note

It is important that the orange juice and evaporated milk are really cold before mixing and that you add the milk last while continuously stirring the juice; otherwise, the milk will curdle.

morir soñando

YIELD 5 servings   PREP TIME 15 minutes

Morir soñando is a true Dominican culinary gem. The name literally translates to "to die dreaming." I couldn't really tell you where the name comes from, but it goes along with the very Dominican custom of giving interesting or funny names to fairly common or simple things and dishes. The traditional version of this cold beverage is made with milk, orange juice, and sugar. It's usually enjoyed as an afternoon snack or whenever you're in the mood for a nice, cold drink.

1½ cups (360 ml) cold fresh orange juice (about 5 oranges) (see Note)

½ cup (100 g) granulated sugar

1 teaspoon vanilla extract (optional)

2 to 3 cups (280 to 420 g) ice cubes

1 can (12 ounces, or 354 ml) cold evaporated milk (see Note)

Orange and/or lime slices, for garnishing

1. In a large pitcher, combine the orange juice, sugar, and vanilla (if using) and stir until the sugar is dissolved.

2. Stir in the ice.

3. Pour in the milk while stirring continuously.

4. Pour into glasses, garnish with orange and/or lime slices, and serve immediately.

morir soñando de limón

lime morir soñando

YIELD 4 servings   **PREP TIME** 15 minutes

A simple variation on the traditional Morir Soñando (page 179), using lime juice instead of orange juice, this version is my mother's and my favorite.

½ cup (120 ml) cold fresh lime juice (4 to 8 limes) (see Note)

¾ cup (150 g) granulated sugar

2 to 3 cups (280 to 420 g) ice cubes

1 can (12 ounces, or 354 ml) cold evaporated milk (see Note)

Lime slices, for garnishing

1 In a large pitcher, combine the lime juice, sugar, and 1 cup (240 ml) of water and stir until the sugar is dissolved.

2 Stir in the ice.

3 Pour in the evaporated milk while stirring continuously.

4 Pour into glasses, garnish with lime slices, and serve immediately.

note *Make sure that the lime juice and evaporated milk are well chilled before pouring the milk into the pitcher. This will prevent the milk from curdling.*

morir soñando de chinola
passion fruit morir soñando

YIELD 5 servings   PREP TIME 15 minutes

Dominicans love a good Morir Soñando (page 179), and although the refreshing juice is traditionally prepared with orange juice, there are a number of variations that taste just as good, if not better. This version substitutes maracuya or chinola (passion fruit) juice for orange juice and is prepared in the same manner as the traditional recipe.

16 ounces (454 g) cold packaged fresh passion fruit pulp (see Note)

¾ cup (150 g) granulated sugar

2 to 3 cups (280 to 420 g) ice cubes

1 can (12 ounces, or 354 ml) cold evaporated milk

1   In a blender, blend the passion fruit pulp and sugar with 1 cup (240 ml) of water for about 1 minute, or until well combined. Pass the mixture through a strainer into a large pitcher to remove broken-down seeds.

2   Stir the ice into the pitcher to make it cold.

3   Slowly pour in the evaporated milk while stirring continuously.

4   Pour into glasses and serve immediately.

note *You can use packaged fresh or frozen passion fruit pulp. If using frozen, add an additional ½ cup (120 ml) of water and only 1 to 2 cups (140 to 280 g) of ice.*

batido de lechosa

papaya shake

YIELD 4 servings   PREP TIME 10 minutes

Batidos are one of the best and most refreshing ways to enjoy some of the delicious exotic fruits widely available in the Caribbean. Tropical fruits are mixed with milk, sugar, and ice to make sweet, refreshing shakes loved by kids and adults alike. Dominicans add a touch of cinnamon and/or nutmeg, giving these shakes a touch of spice that is typical of Dominican cuisine. Batido de lechosa is a favorite that is often served for breakfast or as an afternoon snack. It's common to find this shake on the menu at most cafeterias on the island.

3 cups (450 g) peeled and cubed fresh papaya (see Note)

1 can (12 ounces, or 354 ml) evaporated milk

¼ cup (50 g) granulated sugar, plus more if needed

1 teaspoon vanilla extract

½ teaspoon ground cinnamon

⅛ teaspoon grated or ground nutmeg

1 to 2 cups (140 to 280 g) ice cubes

1   In a blender, blend the papaya, evaporated milk, sugar, vanilla extract, cinnamon, and nutmeg on high speed for 3 to 5 minutes, or until the ice is well blended and smooth.

2   Taste and add more sugar if needed. If you add more sugar, blend for an additional 30 seconds.

3   Pour into glasses and serve immediately.

note
You can also use frozen papaya, which can be found with the Hispanic items in the frozen food section at the grocery store.

batido de zapote

mamey shake

YIELD 4 servings   PREP TIME 10 minutes

Batido de zapote is particularly popular for the sweet and earthy taste of the mamey fruit. The cinnamon is a great complement to this fruit, making the shake even more flavorful. Serve with a Chimichurri (Chimi) Burger (page 42) or Sandwich de Pierna (page 45).

2 cups (300 g) peeled and cubed ripe fresh mamey (zapote) (see Note)

1½ cups (360 ml) whole milk

3 tablespoons granulated sugar, plus more if needed

1 teaspoon vanilla extract

½ teaspoon ground cinnamon

1 to 2 cups (140 to 280 g) ice cubes

1 In a blender, blend the mamey, milk, sugar, vanilla, cinnamon, and ice cubes on high speed for 3 to 5 minutes, or until the ice is well blended and smooth.

2 Taste and add more sugar if needed. If you add more sugar, blend for an additional 30 seconds.

3 Pour into glasses and serve immediately.

note *Ripe mamey is firm but not hard, and if you scratch off some skin close to the stem, it should be a reddish color. If it is green, it is not ripe. You can also use frozen mamey, found with the Hispanic items in the frozen food section at the grocery store.*

batido de guineo
banana shake

YIELD **6 servings**   PREP TIME **10 minutes**

A kid's favorite, batido de guineo is often made with very ripe bananas before they go bad. This refreshing tropical drink is super easy to make and comes together in ten minutes or less. Make it for breakfast or an afternoon snack served with Conconetes (page 165).

3 ripe bananas, peeled

1 teaspoon vanilla extract

5 tablespoons granulated sugar

2 cups (480 ml) whole milk

2 to 3 cups (280 to 420 g) ice cubes

1. In a blender, blend the bananas, vanilla, sugar, milk, and ice cubes for 3 to 5 minutes, or until the ice is well blended and smooth.

2. Pour into glasses and serve immediately.

note *It's best to consume this milkshake immediately and not store it for later, because as it sits, the drink will gel up and lose its freshness.*

note

You can also use a juicer to make this recipe. Simply add the oranges, carrots, and beets to the juicer, then mix the honey (if using) into the juice and refrigerate.

jugo de remolacha, naranja y zanahoria

beet, orange, and carrot juice

YIELD 8 servings   PREP TIME 15 minutes

My grandmother used to make this juice almost every week when I was a kid because it was one of my favorites. When I was pregnant with my son, I craved this juice daily. A close family friend was aware of this and was always delighted to make an entire pitcher just for me. This was fantastic because in addition to being delicious, this juice is also very nutritious. Enjoy it as a refreshing afternoon drink or for breakfast.

6 cups (1.4 L) fresh orange juice (8 to 10 oranges)

2 medium carrots, roughly chopped

1 large beet, peeled and roughly chopped

2 tablespoons honey (optional)

1 In a blender, blend the orange juice, carrots, beet, and honey (if using) on high speed until smooth.

2 Pour the mixture through a strainer into a pitcher to separate the pulp. Discard the pulp. Refrigerate until well chilled.

3 Pour into glasses and serve cold.

jugo de chinola
passion fruit juice

YIELD 4 servings   PREP TIME 15 minutes

Maracuya or chinola (passion fruit) is a tropical fruit typically used in drinks and desserts. Passion fruit juice is a popular cold drink in the Dominican Republic. It's refreshing, natural, and a favorite choice at restaurants and food trucks.

16 ounces (454 g) packaged fresh passion fruit pulp (see Note)

½ cup (100 g) granulated sugar

1 to 2 cups (140 to 280 g) ice cubes

1. In a high-powered blender, blend the passion fruit pulp and sugar with 3 cups (720 ml) of water for about 3 minutes, or until well combined.

2. Pass the mixture through a strainer into a large pitcher to remove broken-down seeds.

3. Serve immediately in tall glasses over the ice or refrigerate until ready to serve.

note

You can use packaged fresh or frozen passion fruit pulp. If using frozen passion fruit, add ½ cup (120 ml) more water when blending to thin it out.

note

You can buy mamajuana mix online. Be sure to get one that contains a mix of some or all these ingredients: palo indio, palo de brasil, canelilla, uña de gato, and spices.

mamajuana

Mamajuana, a drink that is unique to the Dominican Republic, can be found in most markets and tourist resorts on the island. It's a traditional spiced alcoholic beverage made by infusing medicinal leaves, tree bark, herbs, and spices with rum, red wine, and honey. The flavor is mildly sweet, and this fiery drink is said to have numerous benefits ranging from medicinal to aphrodisiacal. If you've been to the Dominican Republic, you've probably tried this drink or brought a bottle home with you.

1 pack (4.6 ounces, or 130 g) mamajuana tree bark mix (see Note)

3 cinnamon sticks, broken into pieces

4 cups (960 ml) hot water

3 cups (720 ml) golden rum, divided

3 cups (720 ml) red wine, divided

½ cup (120 ml) honey, divided

1 In a large, clean bottle or mason jar, place the tree bark mix and cinnamon sticks. Fill the bottle with the hot water, cover with a tight-fitting lid, and let sit for 2 to 3 days. Discard the water.

2 To cure the mamajuana, pour 1½ cups (360 ml) of the rum, 1½ cups (360 ml) of the wine, and ¼ cup (60 ml) of the honey into the bottle, in that order. Cover with a tight-fitting lid and let sit for at least 2 weeks. Strain only the liquid from the bottle and discard.

3 Fill the bottle again with the remaining 1½ cups (360 ml) rum, 1½ cups (360 ml) wine, and ¼ cup (60 ml) honey. Let rest for an additional 1 to 2 weeks.

4 Serve in chilled shot glasses.

avena caliente
hot oat and milk drink

YIELD **4 servings** PREP TIME **5 minutes** COOK TIME **5 minutes**

Few recipes inspire as much comfort as a nice cup of avena caliente does. Often served at the breakfast table, this oatmeal in drink form is made with milk, sugar, and a combination of spices that warm the soul.

½ cup (45 g) rolled oats

4 cups (960 ml) whole milk

⅓ cup (65 g) granulated sugar

¼ teaspoon salt

1 teaspoon vanilla extract

4 cinnamon sticks

⅛ teaspoon ground cloves

⅛ teaspoon grated or ground nutmeg

1 In a blender, blend the oats and milk for 1 to 2 minutes, or until the oats are broken down and nearly dissolved (see Note).

2 Pour the oat-milk mixture into a large pot and bring to a boil over medium-high heat.

3 Once boiling, add the sugar, salt, vanilla, cinnamon sticks, cloves, and nutmeg to the pot. Once it comes to a boil, reduce the heat to low and let simmer slowly for 5 to 10 minutes, or until it begins to thicken and has reduced by about one-quarter.

4 Remove and discard the cinnamon sticks.

5 Ladle into mugs and serve warm.

note

Some people like to strain the oat and milk mixture after blending it to remove some of the oat fibers. You can add this step if you want, but I find that after thoroughly blending the oats, there is no need to strain it.

note

Dominican sweet chocolate tablets sweeten the hot chocolate enough so no sugar needs to be added. If you can't find this chocolate, use semisweet chocolate and add granulated sugar to taste.

chocolate caliente

hot chocolate

YIELD 4 servings   PREP TIME 2 minutes   COOK TIME 15 minutes

One of my abuela's (grandmother's) must-have pantry items was a box of Chocolate Embajador. She used the sweet chocolate tablets to make hot chocolate. My grandmother loved a good hot chocolate, and she would make it often, both for breakfast and dinner. She dipped a fresh pan de agua (a Dominican bread similar to a French baguette) into a cup of sweet hot chocolate and savored every bite of it with the enjoyment of a child having their favorite candy. This recipe is prepared with milk as the base; Dominicans also make chocolate de agua, a water-based hot chocolate that is just as delicious. Enjoy with pan de agua or Conconetes (page 165).

4 cups (960 ml) whole milk

4 ounces (113 g) Dominican sweet chocolate tablets (see Note)

¼ teaspoon ground cinnamon

⅛ teaspoon salt

1 In a medium pot, simmer the milk, chocolate, cinnamon, and salt over medium heat for about 15 minutes, or until the chocolate is completely melted.

2 Ladle into mugs and serve hot.

té de jengibre

ginger tea

YIELD 3 servings   PREP TIME 5 minutes   COOK TIME 15 minutes

Dominicans are famous for their ability to produce a tea that cures all ailments. From headaches to colds, you can bet a Dominican grandmother has a tea for it. Ginger tea is popular not only for its health benefits but also for serving during family gatherings in December when the weather on the island cools down.

½ pound (227 g) fresh ginger

1 cinnamon stick

Honey, granulated sugar, and/or sweetener of choice, for serving

1 Using a wooden spoon, press and squash the ginger to break it up a little bit.

2 To a medium saucepan, add the ginger, cinnamon stick, and 4½ cups (1.1 L) of water. Bring to a boil over medium-high heat, then reduce the heat to medium-low. Let simmer for about 10 minutes. Remove from the heat.

3 Pour the liquid through a mesh strainer before serving.

4 Ladle into mugs and serve with sweetener(s).

note
You can add half of a lemon and/or half of an apple (any kind) to the pot for added flavor and a delicious variation for this ginger tea.

XXXXXXXXXXXXXXXXXXXXXXXXXX

acknowledgments

This book would not have been possible without the recipes, tips, and tricks shared by my family. From Tía Candida's Majarete (page 162), Tía Zoraida's tips to make the perfect Sancocho Dominicano (page 85), my sister Ibly's famous Kipes (page 34), Tía Teresa's Conconetes (page 165)—whose recipe was learned from Great-Grandma Corina and Tía Consuelo—my grandmother Agapita's Sancocho de Habichuelas (page 97), and my mom's Chivo Guisado (page 125), this cookbook is filled with recipes and advice that have transcended generations. I owe my love for food to them.

A special thanks to Erin Canning and the whole team at The Quarto Group for believing in this project and for sharing my excitement about Dominican food.

To my work family, Ana Flores, Roxanna Sarmiento, Melissa Bailey, and the #WeAllGrow Latina team. Knowingly and unknowingly, you all planted the seed and provided the encouragement that led me here.

To my amazing friend Jenny Clater, for capturing a beautiful moment with my mom and me at the farmers market.

To the loyal readers of My Dominican Kitchen, whose emails, comments, and direct messages inspire and motivate me to continue to share the flavors of comida criolla with the world. Thank you for your continued support. This book is for you.

To my children's father, Aneudy Rosado, for taking the portrait photos that capture our everyday family dynamic, for serving as my taste tester during the early days of my cooking journey, and for your constant reassurance that the world wouldn't end if a dish didn't turn out perfect the first time. Your patience keeps me grounded.

A heartfelt thanks to my mother, Veronica Calcaño, and my children, Amelie and Jayden, for being my biggest supporters, for cooking with me, tasting my food, helping me style my shots, holding the reflector, editing my text, and giving me space when needed. I couldn't have done this without you. This book is also yours.

Last, I want to express my gratitude to each and every one of you who takes up this book and prepares a special meal for your family and friends. May you find comfort and joy in every meal.

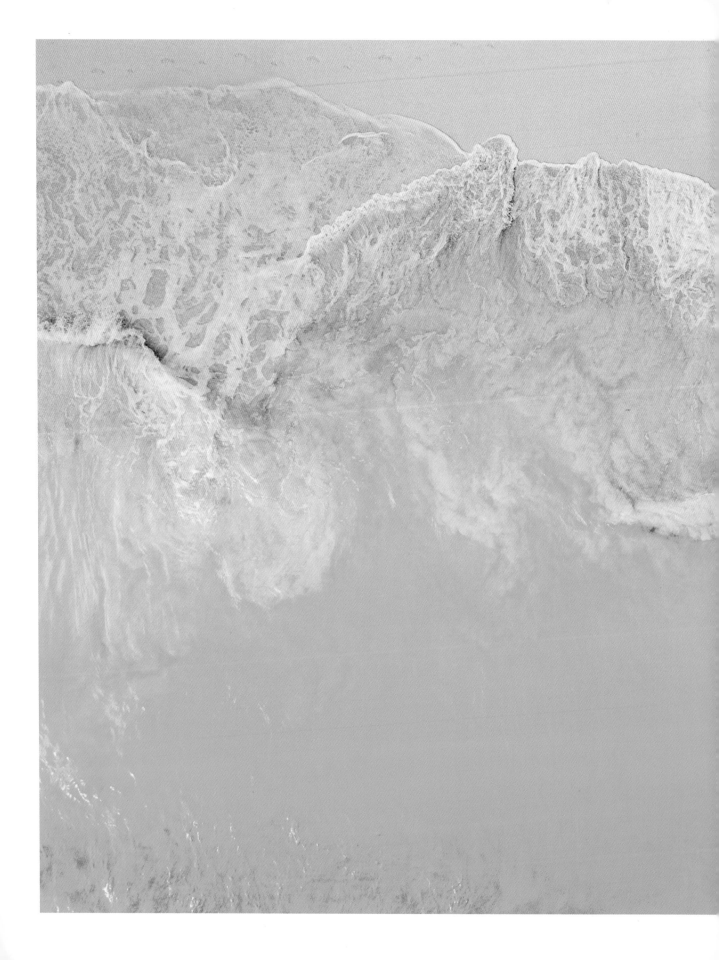

about the author

VANESSA MOTA is an award-winning food photographer and content creator. Her love for food led her to create *My Dominican Kitchen*, a bilingual blog sharing traditional Dominican recipes and Latin-inspired meals for home cooks.

She was born in Santo Domingo, the capital city of the Dominican Republic, and grew up in a matriarchal household surrounded by amazing cooks. Her interest in food began as a child visiting the farmers market with her mom and watching her grandmother and aunts cook delicious traditional Dominican meals. But it wasn't until adulthood that Vanessa learned how to cook, while pregnant with her first child, living in New York City, and missing her family's home cooking.

She started her blog as a way to preserve her family's recipes and share with the world the flavors of la comida criolla (Creole food). She has been recognized as a top food photographer and creator by Hispanicize, BlogHer, and Mom 2.0, and is a member of the 2021 fall class of Cafe Media's Remarkable Voices.

Vanessa lives in northern New Jersey with her two children and their dog, Luna.